D0903340

11·5·79

Modern African Writers
DORIS LESSING'S AFRICA

Gerald Moore, General Editor

Doris Lessing is probably one of the most important and internationally respected white African authors.

Michael Thorpe gives both a critical account of her writings and also some insight into the African context within which they were written. He describes Doris Lessing's feeling for Africa, her treatment of the white experience, her balanced views of social and political matters and her understanding of black/white relationships – the attitudes which have won for her widespread respect.

Doris Lessing's Africa is of particular relevance now, as Rhodesia, her native country, prepares to become the state of Zimbabwe.

DORIS LESSING'S AFRICA

Michael Thorpe
Professor of English, Mount Allison University

**AFRICANA
PUBLISHING
COMPANY**
A division of Holmes & Meier Publishers, Inc.
30 Irving Place, New York, N.Y. 10003

Published by Evans Brothers Limited
Montague House, Russell Square
London WC1B 5BX

Evans Brothers (Nigeria Publishers) Limited
PMB 5164, Jericho Road
Ibadan

First published 1978

Cover illustration by Colin Hawkins

Filmset and printed by
BAS Printers Limited, Over Wallop, Hampshire
Set in 11 on 12 point Ehrhardt
Limp ISBN 0 237 49977 0
Cased ISBN 0 237 49976 2   PRA 6045

To Vernie February
Student, colleague and friend.
Exiled from his Africa.

Contents

Acknowledgements

The publishers acknowledge with thanks permission to reproduce extracts from the following:

The African Voice in Southern Rhodesia by T. O. Ranger, published by Heinemann Educational Books Ltd.; Crisis in Rhodesia by Nathan M. Shamuyarira, published by Andre Deutsch Ltd.; 'The Death of the Moth' from *The Death of the Moth and Other Essays* by Virginia Woolf, published by The Hogarth Press Ltd. and reproduced by permission of the Author's Literary Estate; *Declaration* edited by T. Maschler, published by MacGibbon & Kee Ltd./Granada Publishing Ltd.; *A Humanist in Africa* by Colin Morris, published by Longman; *Rhodesia: The Road to Rebellion* by James Barber, reproduced by permission of the Oxford University Press; *Sounds of a Cowhide Drum* by Oswald Mtshali reproduced by permission of the Oxford University Press; *Tradition and Dream* by Walter Allen, published by J. M. Dent & Sons Ltd.; *The Waste Land* by T. S. Eliot, published by Faber and Faber Ltd.

The publishers are also grateful to Doris Lessing for permission to reproduce extracts from her works.

Editor's foreword

The two white novelists who have written most honestly and perceptively about Africa in our day are Doris Lessing and Nadine Gordimer. The fact that this series is publishing studies of both of them makes some comparison inevitable, and the initial lines of such a comparison are obvious. As Michael Thorpe remarks here, Doris Lessing's lonely, bush childhood; her solitary communing with books and landscape rather than with people; link her more with the Olive Schreiner of *The Story of an African Farm*, written seventy years before *The Grass is Singing*, than with the urban sophistication of Miss Gordimer's upbringing. Like her heroine Martha Quest, Doris Lessing had to fight her way to education, awareness and a degree of self-liberation, from the unpromising platform of a conventional marriage and a provincial ignorance of the world.

These experiences of childhood and youth have left their mark on her work, in the intense self-absorption shown by her heroines, their preoccupation with their own development, and their much higher degree of autobiographical reference, even though they are fully-realized fictional figures.

The creation of male heroes as diverse and as intimately known as Gordimer's Bray (*A Guest of Honour*) or Mehring (*The Conservationist*) would certainly be beyond her scope. Likewise, her African characters never assume the degree of life and verisimilitude we find in Mweta and Shinza, or in Jacobus, in the same two novels. Africans in her work are instrumental to self-discovery in her white characters. But her work displays the obverse of these limitations in her passionate quest for the truth about herself and her relation to society, a society she only really discovered when already a grown girl. It is this searching, introspective quality which has made her work so much emulated and admired in an age absorbed in the discovery of the female psyche, but there is also a core of shrewd, informed realism in her work which makes her an outstanding observer of both the 'Zambesian' and the London scene. Books like *Going Home* display her powers as a political and social commentator, while the same qualities send a tough strand through all her best fiction.

Professor Thorpe ends his study with the virtual abandonment of specifically African material in her work after the mid-sixties. But it is tempting to speculate whether her increasing pre-occupation with disintegration and doom, in recent books like *Briefing for a Descent into Hell* and *Memoirs of a Survivor*, is linked to her continuing status as an outsider in the culture of the West; her conviction that Africa and China are the continents of the future. What appears to be a change of viewpoint may be simply a shifting of her Zambesian eye to new subjects, rather than any alteration in the eye itself.

Gerald Moore

Preface

This brief study of Doris Lessing's writing about Africa is intended as a critical commentary, arranged in the appropriate chronological order of publication of the relevant works, providing whatever additional perspectives – biographical, historical, cultural, seem necessary. The study has been written for the interested *reader* of Lessing's work: I have, therefore, dispensed with the lengthy plot summaries which inflate the pages of all too many critical studies and make them a virtual substitute for the creative works they discuss. Nor have I given much space to differing from other critics of Lessing's work (though I have acknowledged opinions I endorse).

No critic of Lessing, whose distaste for academic literature departments as factories for the mass production of second-hand opinions should be well known, can excuse himself easily for contributing to the ever-growing heap of superfluous criticism. As she writes in her Preface to the Second Edition of *The Golden Notebook*: 'It is possible for literary students to spend more time reading criticism and criticism of criticism than they spend reading poetry, novels, biography, stories.' This is sadly true and no one who publishes criticism of her work should be insensitive to it. His problem, in fact, is to justify publishing criticism of her at all and claiming valuable time for reading it when, as she suggests, the reader would be better advised to spend his efforts on exploring other original works. However, criticism can promote richer reading. It offers the reader *who has read and valued the works themselves* an opportunity to enter into a private dialogue with the critic about their meaning and value; and it can by providing the kinds of perspective I have mentioned above clarify or enlarge the contexts of the work.

This study was written three years ago, in June 1975. Since then the Rhodesian conflict has intensified, and so violent a climax is threatened that, when the new Zimbabwe is proclaimed, it will be

1

yet another botched beginning. Few whites will remain to help build a multi-racial state, and the next phase may be a ruinous tribalism. Lessing's work will remain as chorus to the brief episode that was Rhodesia, a testimony to unexplored possibilities, wasted virtues, thoughtless vices, a quarry for the distant white historian or critic rather than the stuff of the lending libraries of Zimbabwe. Rhodes' grave will be desecrated, and the one lasting reminder of his ill-starred imperialism will be the regular flow to Oxford of Rhodes Scholars whom in his will he had seen as furthering 'the unity of the empire', making 'the performance of public duties [their] highest aim'. Not Rhodes' warped humanism, but Lessing's African writing – for its broad humanity, keen judgement, disciplined style, and its love of the Africa that might be – bequeaths to Africans, black and white, the worthiest memorial of that lightly named land.

A Note on 'Zambesia'

Doris Lessing calls that part of Africa of which she writes 'Zambesia'. Though it is well known that she comes from Southern Rhodesia and knows that country best, she has not wished her African writing to be read in such narrow terms. In a Note to *The Four-Gated City* (p. 711) she makes this clear:

> I used the name Zambesia for the white-dominated colony described in these volumes [*Children of Violence*] because I did not want it to be thought that what I described was peculiar to Southern Rhodesia. My Zambesia is a composite of various white-dominated parts of Africa and, as I've since discovered, some of the characteristics of its white people are those of any ruling minority whatever their colour.

Her usage corresponds largely with that of Ronald Robinson and John Gallagher who, following the common usage among whites in the early colonial period, use 'Zambesia' in *Africa and the Victorians* (1961) to denote the territories of the central basin of the Zambezi and Limpopo Rivers, lying to the north of the Limpopo, to the west of Lake Nyasa and to the south and east of the old Congo Free State, the River Zambezi dividing northern from southern Zambesia. This covers, in addition to Southern Rhodesia, the former Northern Rhodesia (now Zambia) and Nyasaland (now Malawi), territories which Lessing would in the 'fifties have included among the white-dominated parts of Africa, together with those in East Africa at that time and the Union of South Africa.

2

1   Introduction

Doris Lessing has become the most widely recognized and most seriously considered woman novelist writing in English since Virginia Woolf died in 1941. Unlike Woolf, she has not made remarkable advances in the form of the novel, but has greatly extended its subject-matter, notably in that very sphere in which Woolf had felt herself to be wanting: 'telling the truth about my own experiences as a body . . . I doubt that any woman has solved it yet'.[1] It is for her strenuous attempts to 'solve' this, in such massive works as *The Golden Notebook* and *The Four-Gated City*, that Lessing is now most widely discussed and admired: for this, and her more recently developed exploration of extreme mental states, traversing the misty border between 'sanity' and 'insanity' – a preoccupation which *continues* one of Virginia Woolf's heartfelt concerns. These two leading women novelists of the past sixty years, in so many ways worlds – as well as generations – apart, do come together in this: that they have focused upon the inner life as the source and test of what we are and what we achieve in the outer life of society. (Whether this is a particularly feminine strength is the kind of question I prefer to avoid discussing here.)

Doris Lessing's first world is infinitely remote from Virginia Woolf's liberal middle-class origins and upbringing in London as a member of a highly cultured late Victorian family, one of *the* intellectual families of her time. Lessing's is the world of the 'Colonial', far removed not only from the metropolitan centre of culture, but from any strong cultural influence. In these respects, until very recently, the 'Colonial' world generally was seen from the mother country as second class, dependent, and this was how it might see itself – though aggressively protesting it was as good as the mother country, if not better. For the intelligent and sensitive girl growing up in such a world in the 'twenties, as for many

---

[1] V. Woolf, *The Death of a Moth* (1942), Penguin Books 1961, p. 206.

'Colonial' writers before and since, it was necessary to make her own world. Nothing was given, little inherited. An English novelist like Virginia Woolf, when she began writing, did so with an inevitable consciousness of those – George Eliot, the Brontës, Jane Austen – who had gone before and wrestled with the same language, the same society, the same landscapes. If Doris Lessing has no such bearings to steer by, nor was she overshadowed by her predecessors. It could be 'her' Africa.

It could also be 'her' Africa in another sense which, if we are to learn to understand Africa from its ever-growing band of writers, needs careful identification. There is no more one Africa than there is one Europe, one America – but it is harder for the African writer than for his European counterpart to feel that he participates in a culture of continental scope. This is as hard for the African tribesman as for the white settler. The African writer has been, so far, predominantly a regional or tribal writer: we link Amos Tutuola with Nigerian Yoruba culture, Chinua Achebe with Igboland, James Ngugi with the Gikuyu of Kenya. Amongst the European settlers Isak Dinesen (Karen Blixen) is indissolubly linked with the airy highlands of Kenya, Olive Schreiner with the Cape Karroo of South Africa, Doris Lessing with Southern Rhodesia (see Prefatory Note on 'Zambesia') whose first, and still only, significant writer she is. The landscape, its people – both blacks and settlers – its modern history and society, in which she spent most of her first thirty years, are the subject-matter of a major part of her writing. Even today, after twenty-five years in London, her Africa has not ceased to inspire her.

She was brought to Rhodesia at the age of five. She had been born and lived until that time in Persia, where her father Alfred Cook Tayler had managed a branch for the Imperial Bank of Persia. Like many other Englishmen who had fought and lived through the horrors and disillusionment of the Great War, he was restlessly on the look-out for a new, independent life. He saw a seemingly golden opportunity for this in the Rhodesian inducements to settlers advertised at the Empire Exhibition in London which he visited when on leave from Persia in 1925. It had been made possible for white (mostly British) settlers to acquire huge farms on easy terms from the colonial government, the government having first ejected Africans from the land and crowded them into 'reserves'. The going price was ten shillings an acre and Alfred Cook Tayler took up 3000 acres of it (actually a comparatively modest spread). To this in 1925 he took out his family, his daughter, her brother (two and a half years younger than Doris), and the wife who had nursed him when he was seriously wounded in the War (a leg was amputated to the thigh) and whom he had afterwards married:

> Soon, there was my father in a cigar-shaped house of thatch and mud on the top of a *kopje* that overlooked in all directions a great system of mountains, rivers, valleys, while overhead the sky arched from horizon to empty horizon. This was a couple of hundred miles south from the Zambesi, a hundred or so west from Mozambique, in the district of Banket, so called because certain of its reefs were of the same formation as those called banket on the Rand. Lomagundi – gold country, tobacco country, maize country, wild, almost empty. (The Africans had been turned off it into Reserves.) Our neighbours were four, five, seven miles off. In front of the house no neighbours, nothing; no farms, just wild bush with two rivers but no fences to the mountains seven miles away. And beyond these mountains and bush again to the Portuguese border over which 'our boys' used to escape when wanted by the police for pass or other offences.[1]

Banket is in Mashonaland, the homeland of a tribe threatened first by the Matabele and then by the white settlers under thrusting Empire-builder Cecil Rhodes who, after making a dubious treaty with Lobengula and his Matabele and crushing the Mashona uprising of 1896, began to 'alienate' (the ironically apt technical term) the best of what land remained to the tribesmen:[2]

> He grazed cattle on it. He cultivated about 300 acres of his land; the rest was left unused. He employed between 50 and a 100 black men, and their wages were 12s. 6d. a month, with rations of maize meal, beans and a little meat. (Maize was introduced by the white people as a cheap filling food for the blacks.) The labourers came from the Reserves, Nyasaland, Portuguese territory. They built themselves a mud hut in the 'compound'. They were given a day to do this. *The Second Hut* [in *This Was the Old Chief's Country*] describes how such a

---

[1] 'All Seething Underneath', *Vogue*, 15 February 1964, p. 132: an article devoted to memoirs of DL's father (1886–1946). Another amusing and affectionate sketch of her father and a shrewd analysis of his 'Englishness' may be found in *In Pursuit of the English*, Chapter 1.

[2] This was a gradual process, still continuing into the 'thirties, as is witnessed in retrospect by the story of 'The Old Chief Mshlanga' in *This Was the Old Chief's Country* (1951). (See Chapter 3.)

hut is built. They worked from six in the morning till six at night with an hour off at midday, seven days a week in the busy season. These were the conditions of the whole country: my father was a better, more humane employer than most. But no one can be more humane than an economic framework allows one to be.[1]

Growing up on the lonely farm on the high veld between the wars the young Doris had little racial consciousness and only a slowly dawning understanding of the true relations between her people and the blacks. Southern Rhodesia, like the rest of British Africa, was very far from being a 'cause'. She had the freedom and space to live that largely solitary childhood (her brother being away at school much of the time) which makes for introspection, dreaming, a close fellowship with the natural surroundings, a freedom from early intellectual involvement. Similar conditions have nourished the imagination of so many individualistic writers – 'colonial' writers like Olive Schreiner and Henry Handel Richardson (Ethel Florence Lindesay), Schreiner's Australian contemporary, suggest a close affinity.

Doris Lessing escaped much of the child's usual sentence in the 'prison house' of school, a convent school in Salisbury, the colonial capital, where she seems to have been found a 'difficult' or 'neurotic' child. After fourteen she had no formal schooling. For about two years she worked in Salisbury as a nursemaid, or what nowadays might in England be called an 'au pair' girl, then returned to the family farm. There she wrote some 'bad novels' and destroyed them, before returning to Salisbury in 1938 to work as a telephone operator; she was then eighteen.

This was shortly before the Second World War broke out. She found herself in an ingrown, intensely race- and class-conscious colonial society. At first, if we may read some general autobiographical elements into her portrayal of Martha Quest, the heroine of her 'Children of Violence' novels, she went with the stream: first a frenetic 'good time', then 'a proper marriage' with a colonial civil servant. Of this marriage a boy and a girl were born, but it ended in divorce in 1943: out of a natural consideration for those involved (and still living) Mrs. Lessing has preferred to give no further details about that period of her life.

The War precipitated alien influences into the settler society of

[1]DL's Introduction to *Nine African Stories*, ed. M. Marland (Longmans 1968), p. 7.

Southern Rhodesia and disturbed its ingrown conservatism. For Doris Lessing herself most important were the contacts it brought with young Englishmen sent out to serve in the Royal Air Force bases there. They brought with them what was then the fresh Marxist idealism of the 'thirties: they soon formed a Communist group, in which there were no distinctions of race, which she joined:

> There was a time in my life when I was a member of a Communist group which was pure – they had no contact with any kind of reality! It must have been blessed by Lenin from his grave, it was so pure . . . for a period of about three years, a group of enormously idealistic and mostly extremely intellectual people created a Communist party in a vacuum which no existing Communist party anywhere in the world would have recognized as such.[1]

The English servicemen who formed this group were a completely new element in the claustrophobic Rhodesian society, men quite untouched by the attitudes typical of an outnumbered 'superior race', the bearers of the seeds of the (then) most appealing new Western faith. Other newcomers included refugees from Hitler's Europe, one of whom Gottfried Lessing, also a communist, she married in 1945. This marriage also ended in divorce in 1949. In the same year she left Rhodesia and came, with the son born of the second marriage, to try her literary fortunes in London. She has lived there ever since.

Lessing's involvement in leftist politics continued for some years after she left Rhodesia and supplies a major theme in the 'Children of Violence' series from the second book, *A Proper Marriage*, onwards. Though she did join the British Communist Party, it would be a mistake to interpret that as a strong commitment. She only joined three years after she came to England – establishing herself there as a writer must have been her first task – and left it in 1956. Nor did she leave in that year, as many did, simply out of revulsion at the Russian invasion of Hungary: as many had found before her, the British Communist Party had never been the most inspiring of its kind; in any case, it is impossible to imagine so open-minded a creative writer fitting herself readily to such a party's shufflings and compromises. Before her fiction began to deal

[1] 'A Talk with Doris Lessing', interview by Florence Howe, *The Nation*, 204, 6 March 1967, p. 312.

explicitly with communism, it was already firmly grounded in a strong humanitarian, not a narrowly political, concern with 'man's inhumanity to man' as she had seen it in the white's unjust dealing with the African.[1]

This concern brought her back to Rhodesia in 1956 for rediscovery and reassessment in the light of the new political perspectives of the 'winds of change' period: 'I needed to see how Rhodesia struck me after living in a civilised country. But "emotional reasons" were equally strong: I needed to feel and smell the place.'[2] Ironically, as her rueful concluding pages to *Going Home* record, she did the trip on belated royalties due from Russia and sent to that country articles which, though 'anti-imperialist' enough in their own right, were nevertheless hacked about by State censorship. It must have been her last act for the Party. It also brought her the by no means despicable notoriety of being declared a Prohibited Immigrant by the then Federation Government and by the South African government. No reasons were given: it is by such arbitrary acts that the distinction once claimed by the Rhodesian government, of a greater openness than its neighbour South Africa, has been shown to be hollow. *Going Home* is a sad and bitter indictment of a Rhodesian contempt for and exploitation of the African, a contempt worsened, if that were possible, by the hypocritical pretence that the 'British' Rhodesian Government was really more enlightened than that of the Union.

By the time of her banning in August 1956 Doris Lessing had become the strongest English writer against white oppression in Central and Southern Africa. *The Grass is Singing* (1950) had made an immediate impact, and it had been quickly followed by two volumes of short stories, *This Was the Old Chief's Country* (1951), *Five* (1953), and the first two books of the 'Children of Violence' sequence, *Martha Quest* (1952) and *A Proper Marriage* (1954). In all these works her unsentimental grasp of the political and social realities and her depth of insight into white and black alike gave her a strength far beyond the reach of her best-known forerunners amongst critics of apartheid: Alan Paton, whose *Cry, the Beloved Country* had led the way in 1944, and Peter Abrahams.

While 'the colour problem' is an inevitable theme in her work, Lessing has no more wished her writing to be tied to that than to

[1] In her interview with C. J. Drwer, *The New Review* (November 1974), Lessing brings out clearly the nature and limits of her Communist connection and expresses her disenchantment with political solutions to social problems.
[2] *Going Home* (Panther Books, Revised edition 1968), p. 314.

Marxist ideology. In the Preface to her first collected *African Stories* (1964) she recalls how reviewers had described her early books 'as about the colour problem . . . which is not how I see, or saw, them . . . while the cruelties of the white man towards the black man are amongst the heaviest counts in the indictment against humanity, colour prejudice is not our original fault, but only one aspect of the atrophy in the imagination that prevents us from seeing ourselves in every creature that breathes under the sun'. (It would not surprise her, unlike some blinkered 'liberals', that members of rival factions amongst black Zimbabwe freedom movements are now destroying each other.) It is an open-eyed understanding of humanity, across the lines of colour, society or place, which has from the beginning rendered her African writings at one and the same time intensely African and yet the source of a wider insight into the general human condition.

Inevitably, this breadth of hers – not just the fact of 'exile' – was bound to lead Lessing beyond purely African subject-matter. Her first larger attempt to expand her range, *Retreat to Innocence* (1956), a romantic novel set in London, was, however, her one conspicuous failure. That lapse was redeemed and obliterated by *The Golden Notebook* (1962), perhaps her best-known single work for its comprehensive presentation of an intelligent and sensitive contemporary woman's experience. Inevitably, though not intentionally, a major original contribution to the now burgeoning literature of the 'free woman', it is largely and successfully set in London, but includes a strong strand of African narrative in the form of flashbacks. By the time she brought her 'Children of Violence' sequence to a conclusion, with *The Four-Gated City* (1969), the setting was almost wholly London, but an 'Appendix' – to which the author attaches great importance – pushes forward into an African future. Since 1969, apart from the title story in the collection *The Story of a Non-Marrying Man* (1972), Africa has seemingly disappeared from her sources of creativity. Yet she has written as recently as 1972, of her African stories: 'Time has nothing to do with it. A certain kind of pulse starts beating, and I recognize it: it is time I wrote another story from that landscape, external and internal at the same time, which was once the Old Chief's Country.'[1]

She may at any time return in her imagination to Africa. Surely

[1]Preface to *The Sun Between Their Feet*, Volume Two of DL's Collected African Stories (Michael Joseph, London, 1973), p. 9.

she is indirectly doing so in the settings of parts of such recent novels as *Briefing for a Descent into Hell* (1971) and *The Summer Before the Dark* (1973), in the (surely African) sun motif that pervades *Briefing*, in the recurrence in the novel of the ideal city which Martha Quest had envisioned twenty years before – and which the author so passionately clings to:

> The yellow flanks of Africa lie beneath the moving insect-like plane, black-maned with forest, twitching in the heat. A magnificent country, with all its riches in the future. Because it is so empty we can dream. We can dream of cities and a civilization more beautiful than anything that has been seen in the world before.[1]

The following pages will attempt to explore Doris Lessing's Africa as dream and reality.

[1]*Going Home*, op. cit., pp. 13–14.

2   The Grass is Singing

In 1949 Doris Lessing brought her African experience and African writing to London at a timely moment. The African question was emerging and the 'fifties were to be a period of violent transition throughout the continent, from the Congo to Kenya, from Algeria to Nigeria. It is one of the unintentional ironies of *The Grass is Singing*, then and since one of the most telling literary portents of that change, that it should be set in a country which today is one of the two barely surviving enclaves of white minority rule in Africa.

The novel was published in 1950, after being accepted by the first English publishers the author approached. (Surprisingly, one South African publisher accepted it, but on unsatisfactory terms.) It was reprinted seven times in five months; by 1971 the Penguin edition alone had sold 70,000 copies. Reviewers at once acclaimed it as the most promising novel to have appeared in England since the Second World War and certainly it was the most successful colonial novel since *The Story of an African Farm* surprised London in 1883. (It was not a high period in the English novel.) Certainly the moment was right, but *The Grass is Singing* was not merely a political novel. It does not deal in ideologies, set black and white issues in opposition or make angry avowals of the author's distaste for white racism or of her support for African self-determination. Not that it cannot be used as a quarry to yield evidence for such attitudes, for there are authorial comments that do point up the social and racial issues for the uninformed reader, but one of its chief strengths is that it is not an attitudinizing work. Lessing's method is to present relationships and an episode and allow readers the liberty of their own interpretation. In characterizing the settlers both in the novel and in her stories she knows that the subject-matter itself is explicit enough.

No one could be further removed from the compassionate and aspiring 'free woman' of the Martha Quest novels that follow than Lessing's protagonist, Mary Turner. We might describe her as a

11

non-heroine. She is commonplace, almost characterless, a weak-willed insecure creature. The man she desirelessly links herself with, in a feeble attempt to break out of the deadly routine of small town colonial society, is another broken reed. The pathos and futility of these two mismatched people's lives, the stale chapters of a flimsy marriage as well as the empty posturings of their socially conditioned white dominance, are conveyed with a delicate faithfulness to their essential blindness to the greater possibilities of their humanity. Into their relationship, which would have otherwise declined into a sterile passivity, the black servant Moses intrudes, not as a mere symbol of colour conflict, but as the agent of a disruptive life force.

In the social context, of course, as seen through the eyes of a Charlie Slatter or the Police Sergeant – the first, *external* view of the situation that opens the narrative – it is a colour issue. The 'love that dares not speak its name' in this context is, not homosexuality, but love across the colour lines: it is the subject of 'the stock South African conversation', as Lessing reports in *Going Home*.[1] This theme had already taken hold as early as William Plomer's *Turbott Wolfe* (1925), but only with *The Grass is Singing* does it acquire the force of a dark archetype.[2] In apparently lusting after her black servant Mary Turner is seen as lowering herself and the race that every single white must represent, yet none of the revolted whites grasps the inner nature of the relationship. Moses' impact upon Mary is physical and emotional; it is only through the developing sexual relationship – in which Mary's true passivity comes out – that the racial roles become reversed. It is thus that we as readers experience it; we can *see* and understand how by slow degrees she is drawn into an ever closer 'personal relationship' with one of the faceless many upon whom she, in common with the poorest and least successful of her race, depends to prop up the material edifice of her life. How physical this relationship becomes, the text never

[1]Op. cit., p. 25.
[2]Developed in many later South African novels, e.g., Peter Abrahams' *Path of Thunder* (1952); the theme reaches tragic intensity in *Looking on Darkness* (1974) by Afrikaans novelist, André Brink. The novels I have mentioned here typically cast the 'illicitly' loved one as female: there is no doubt that white racists find the relationship Lessing chose to describe especially odious. (The white's African mistress is, of course, a commonplace and has been romanticized from Conrad on, though not by Lessing, cf. the stories '"Leopard" George' and 'The Black Madonna', discussed in Chapter 3.) Since 1903 in Rhodesia it has been a criminal offence for a black man and white woman to have sexual intercourse but no such law applies where a white man and a black woman are involved.

tells us; there is no reason even to suppose Lessing herself 'knows'. If she is writing from within her character, a credible interpretation is that Mary's derangement is not the consequence of her breaking the ultimate 'taboo' but rather an unconscious evasion of the step her forbidden desire would take if it could.

A few reviewers criticized Lessing's portrayal of the 'boy' Moses as vague and shadowy. Undoubtedly, this portrayal is suggestive rather than explicit. We see Moses almost entirely through the eyes of Mary and other whites who 'colour' him in accordance with their prejudices and apprehensions. Seen from these angles his depiction is necessarily vague: he is a reflector of white responses. When he acts, to kill Mary, perhaps out of jealousy aroused by the coming of 'his enemy', the new white assistant Marston, we should see that he is stepping outside the character they have stamped upon him and his kind. His passive, African role – in which he had borne Mary's blows – is momentarily shed and he is as human, self-defining, as his white masters. It is they, not the author, who languidly debate 'why the murderer had given himself up' in one of the book's most acid passages; perhaps, theorizes the District Native Commissioner, he was reverting to the traditional customs of Lobengula's time and submitting to his rightful punishment for '. . . an unforgivable thing, like touching one of the King's women . . . (. . . it is permissible to glorify the old ways sometimes, providing one says how depraved the natives have become since.)'[1]

This again is the *external* view with which the book opens; the author quickly points out that it will not do, since Moses 'might not have been a Matabele at all' but just one of many migratory natives from neighbouring tribes. At the end of the book, after we have followed the relationship and witnessed the murder, when Moses steps back in his closing shadows and resigns all attempt to flee, it seems that whatever need drove him is appeased and that it is no part of his creator's business to probe his mind:

> . . . what thoughts of regret, or pity, or perhaps even wounded human affection were compounded with the satisfaction of his completed revenge, it is impossible to say. For, when he had gone perhaps a couple of hundred yards through the soaking bush, he stopped, turned aside, and leaned against a tree on an ant-heap. And there he would remain, until his pursuers, in their turn, came to find him.

[1] *The Grass is Singing*, Penguin edition (1961), p. 13.

These are the novel's closing words, admirably restrained – all the more so that, though we recognize the Conradian note of speculation upon the incomprehensible workings of the 'native' mind, the prose is coolly free of the strained rhetoric with which Conrad was prone to mar such passages.

Perhaps Moses' triumph, savoured after the killing, would have been tinged beyond the hurt of spurned love or possession with a sense of the black man's revenge. We may suppose so, but would be wrong to dwell upon it. However Moses may see them, we see the Turners from the outset as alternately despicable and pathetic members of a spurious master race. Their vulnerability is human, though, and personal; no means of scoring points on the colour issue. They are ordinary, ignorant, fearful, self-centred people, unwitting players on a stage in history whose meaning as spectacle the reader is far better able than they to discern. Mary Turner's passion is not to be a *memsahib*, or to emulate the Tant' Annas of the formidable Boer hegemony to the South, but to find rest and security through marriage – a fragile illusion she *does* share with the more complex women who succeed her in Lessing's fiction: it is always the personal, emotional element that comes first. Dick Turner, the flimsy reed she would lean upon, is no more self-sufficient than she, in Lessing's fiction the first of many fated dreamers in an uncompromising country that yields only to the fighter:

> Dick often stood at the edge of the field, watching the wind flow whitely over the tops of the shining young trees, that bent and swung and shook themselves all day. He had planted them apparently on an impulse; but it was really the fruition of a dream of his . . . It wasn't much, planting a hundred acres of good trees that would grow into straight white-stemmed giants; but it was a small retribution; and this was his favourite place on the farm. When he was particularly worried, or had quarrelled with Mary, or wanted to think clearly, he stood and looked at his trees; or strolled down the long aisles between light swaying branches that glittered with polished leaves like coins.[1]

– and these 'coins' are the only currency his farm yields in profusion. Dick loves the land and will not violate it, unlike Charlie Slatter (the character who conforms most closely to the expected

[1] Ibid., pp. 90–91.

stereotype of the exploiting white); it is that, not the 'lazy savage', to which he feels a debt of 'retribution'. Unquestioningly, he puts the native's labour in service of 'his' trees, his land. In his case it is no crass white exploitation: a romantic like him would have used others to serve his dream whatever their colour. It would be naïve to feel surprise at so 'sensitive' a man's indifference to his kind; such a contradiction is one of the universal enigmas of man's nature. Dick Turner is the first character to embody another contradiction Lessing will return to often: how an intense love of Africa can coexist with a callous or careless indifference to its people. It is because there are such contradictions that Dick can appeal beyond simple oppositions at least to our pity and that even Mary can rise in her trance of imminent death to the compassionate mood in which the author herself has written:

> At last, from a height, she looked down on the building set among the bush – and was filled with a regretful, peaceable tenderness. It seemed as if she were holding that immensely pitiful thing, the farm with its inhabitants, in the hollow of her hand, which curved round it to shut out the gaze of the cruelly critical world.[1]

But every truth is two-faced; in her fear and loathing of it Mary has endowed the bush with an almost human malevolence: after the Turners' departure the house 'would be killed by the bush, which had always hated it . . . the grass would spring up'.[2] But Mary feels drawn toward it, fatalistically, and when she actually walks there on her last morning, oppressed by the shrieking of the cicadas, sets her eyes upon these indifferent tormentors for the first time. The sense of the overmastering bush in this passage gives her a foretaste of her own extinction:

> The trees hated her, but she could not stay in the house. She entered them, feeling the shade fall on her flesh, hearing the cicadas all about, shrilling endlessly, insistently. She walked straight into the bush, thinking: 'I will come across *him*, and it will all be over.' She stumbled through swathes of pale grass, and the bushes dragged at her dress. She leaned at last against a tree, her eyes shut, her ears filled with noise, her

---

[1] Ibid., p. 201. Cf. Lessing's Preface to *African Stories*: 'Africa . . . gives you the knowledge that man is a small creature, among other creatures, in a large landscape.'
[2] Ibid., pp. 206–7.

skin aching. There she remained, waiting, waiting. But the noise was unbearable! She was caught up in a shriek of sound. She opened her eyes again. Straight in front of her was a sapling, its greyish trunk knotted as if it were an old gnarled tree. But they were not knots. Three of those ugly little beetles squatted there, singing away, oblivious of her, of everything, blind to everything but the life-giving sun. She came close to them, staring. Such little beetles to make such an intolerable noise! And she had never seen one before. She realized, suddenly, standing there, that all those years she had lived in that house, with the acres of bush all around her, and she had never penetrated into the trees, had never gone off the paths. And for all those years she had listened wearily, through the hot dry months, with her nerves prickling, to that terrible shrilling, and had never seen the beetles who made it. Lifting her eyes she saw she was standing in the full sun, that seemed so low she could reach up a hand and pluck it out of the sky: a big red sun, sullen with smoke. She reached up her hand; it brushed against a cluster of leaves, and something whirred away. With a little moan of horror she ran through the bushes and the grass, away back to the clearing. There she stood still, clutching at her throat.[1]

She had feared, and almost willed, meeting Moses there. It is not until night that he comes, out of the dark and rain, the lightning that portends violent change; he seizes and begins choking her – 'And then the bush avenged itself; that was her last thought'.[2] This is her atonement, with the bush, the Africa she has held outside full awareness – where indeed she had tried to push Moses, who becomes now, as it were, the avenging spirit of the bush. Perhaps this is her nearest approach to knowing 'what to do with this personal relation'.[3] Moses becomes an almost superstitiously conceived symbol of an abused African reality of which Mary (and this gives her a redeeming interest) approaches tragic understanding.

The long passage quoted above is the one most strongly reminiscent of the novel's title and its manifold suggestiveness. This can be traced back to the whole passage from 'What the Thunder Said', Part V of T. S. Eliot's *The Waste Land* from which

[1] Ibid., pp. 208–9.
[2] Ibid., p. 217.
[3] Ibid., p. 162.

the title is drawn, as quoted in the first of the novel's two epigraphs. The imagery of oppressive heat and dryness in Eliot's poem, symbolizing spiritual dearth, and its disturbing opposite – the awakening thunder and rain – are echoed in the final chapter (though the heat and dryness have built up throughout); Eliot's 'jungle' corresponds to the menacing 'bush'. We see in these parallels Lessing's broader aim, to paint the sterility of white civilization in Africa and the inevitability of violent change – in which the 'dark attraction' of Moses is only a straw in the wind – before there can be new life.[1] As her second epigraph indicates, she may also have borrowed from Eliot the idea of portraying the civilization's weaknesses through its misfits and through sexual inadequacy and maladjustment; Eliot's displaced beings, too, 'can connect / Nothing with nothing'.[2] The affinity between Eliot and Lessing is one of spirit and perception; there is no stylistic debt, nothing in Lessing like Eliot's fragmentary method or elaborate web of allusion. There is poetic intensity, as in the passage last quoted, but the novel never becomes pure symbol or mere thesis, largely because (to use Conrad's terms from the Preface to *The Nigger of the 'Narcissus'*) Lessing's task, like his, is 'by the power of the written word to make you hear, to make you feel – it is, before all, to make you *see*' – in her case to feel that Africa which is as potent a source of attraction and repulsion as the human conflict it includes, and with an intensity comparable to Conrad's own in *Heart of Darkness* (which, in its turn, was a point of allusion for Eliot).

Seen as a whole, *The Grass is Singing* is an ironic yet compassionate exposure of the fragility and futility of the myths upon which white settler society has sustained itself:

> The myths of this society are not European. They are of the frontiersman and the lone-wolf; the brave white woman home-making in lonely primitive conditions; the child who gets himself an education and so a status beyond his parents; the simple and brave savage defeated after gallant fighting on both sides; the childlike and lovable servant; the devoted welfare-worker spending his or her life uplifting backward peoples.[3]

[1] It is perhaps fanciful to see in Lessing, as in Eliot, a concealed allusion to the biblical Moses' smiting of the rocks of the desert to bring forth the waters of salvation; however, the choice of name seems ironically apt.

[2] *The Waste Land*, Part III, ll. 301–2.

[3] *Going Home*, op. cit., p. 65.

This was written, as a summing-up, in 1956, but its point is implicit in the novel of six years before: that ideas of racial superiority last only as long as the myths that feed them work for the myth-makers and are accepted by the subservient. The unheroic Turners are no representatives of a master race, but most convincingly human and vulnerable members of it and themselves portents of its inevitable defeat. In *Going Home* the account of the moral deterioration of the Whartons, the poor white family in Salisbury, is another such portent, perhaps a more up-to-date one.[1] They represent the thousands who have come out to Rhodesia, not to farm and be (albeit precariously) their own masters, but to exchange an overcrowded urban life in England for what turns out to be a very slightly advantaged urban existence in an embattled white enclave in Africa: '. . . what is happening is that the poorer of the white people are becoming more and more like the poorer of the Africans.'[2]

Poverty and insecurity are the true masters: they impoverish the inner life, and it is this the novelist can reveal, going beyond the hard lines of the label and the slogan and proving their hollowness more profoundly than volumes of political analysis and pro-testation. Not that there has been a surplus of protest writing in, or about the Rhodesian situation: it is much needed, and not before it has done its work and the inevitable harsh transformation has come about is the broader vision of *The Grass is Singing* (which I have tried to bring out here) likely to be seen in its true perspective by either of the races involved.

[1] Ibid., p. 238 ff.
[2] Ibid., p. 25. (See in Chapter 6, pp. 76–7, comment on the relationship in *Landlocked* between white trades unionists and Africans.)

3 The Short Stories

The Grass is Singing inaugurated almost a decade of intensive writing about Africa. The stories and novels of stored experience that follow have an unevenness that is hardly surprising in such an outpouring, in a writer moreover so anxious to show and enlighten – and not least in one who was writing for a living, to establish herself as a professional. With very few exceptions, however, the stories that are the subject of this chapter show her at her best as an artist. They share with *The Grass is Singing* a clarity and sureness of aim and execution that lend them a cohesiveness and intensity of effect sometimes lacking in her many-purposed longer fiction.

Lessing's first collection of African stories, *This Was the Old Chief's Country*, was published in 1951. In 1953 five longer stories, or short novels, appeared under the title *Five*. Three of these latter, 'A Home for the Highland Cattle', 'Eldorado' and 'The Antheap', were grouped with *This Was the Old Chief's Country* (again under that title) to make up Volume One of her *Collected African Stories* (1973). The other African story from *Five*, 'Hunger', was grouped with the remaining short stories which had been scattered in several volumes, *The Habit of Loving* (1957), *A Man and Two Women* (1963) and *The Story of a Non-Marrying Man* (1972), to make up Volume Two of the *Collected African Stories*, which also appeared in 1973 under the title of one of her favourite stories, *The Sun Between Their Feet*. Though two pieces, 'The Story of a Non-Marrying Man' and 'Spies I Have Known', appeared as recently as 1972, the African stories belong almost entirely to the early and mid-'fifties, the period during which the first three books of the 'Children of Violence' sequence came out – in 1952, 1954 and 1958.[1] This period, 1950–8, may truly be called her 'African'

---

[1] The two volumes of *Collected African Stories* superseded *African Stories* (1964), but were larger by only two stories from *The Story of a Non-Marrying Man*, bringing the total to 32.

period, when her work drew most intensively upon her African experience and involvement. These bearings given, for the sake of some sense of chronological order, it seems unnecessary to attempt a more detailed dating but rather to endorse the author's comments in her Preface to Volume Two of the *Collected African Stories*:

> In what order has one written this or that?
>
> This seems to be a question of much interest to scholars. I don't see why. No one who understands anything about how artists work – and there is surely no excuse not to, since artists of all kinds write so plentifully about our creative processes – could ask such a question at all. You can think about a story for years, and then write it down in an hour. You may work out the shape of a novel for decades, before spending a few months working on it.

In this chapter, partly for convenience' sake, partly because Lessing does distinguish stylistically between her two kinds of story, I shall discuss the short stories and reserve the four long ones from *Five* for Chapter 4.

A comprehensive reading of the stories provides one with a many-sided, complex picture of life in that part of Africa their author dubs 'Zambesia'. There is no exclusive focus, certainly no imposed didacticism: people, white and black, relationships, place, the flora and fauna – often perceived with a child's lonely, concentrated gaze – make up a living mosaic uncircumscribed by narrow intention. We know from the more evidently personal stories that Africa is the author's element, however it may appear to some of her characters less attuned to it. It is not surprising that the story in which the narrator contemplates the dung beetles' arduous, futile day's labour *against* nature, 'The Sun Between Their Feet', should have been one of the author's favourites. An unsentimental curiosity, a passionate attention to every form and scene of natural life, accepted for what it is, lends her stories a firm, underlying viewpoint. (It is, incidentally, an attitude she shares with Hardy, one of the few English writers whose kinship she has acknowledged.) This is the outgrowth, we can think, not only of quiet observation, but of excited confrontation such as the boy experiences in 'A Sunrise on the Veld' when he goes hunting at dawn beyond the ordered boundaries of the farm. 'Soon he had left the cultivated part of the farm. Behind him the bush was low and black. In front was a long vlei, acres of long pale grass that sent back a hollowing gleam of light to a satiny sky. Near him the thick swathes of grass were bent with the weight of water, and diamond drops sparkled on each frond.'[1] A sense of liberty and joy seizes him and he feels, momentarily, master of life. 'A vision came to him, as he stood there, like when a child hears the word 'eternity' and tries to understand it, and time takes possession of the mind . . . there is nothing I can't become, nothing I can't do; there is no country in the world I cannot make part of myself, if I choose. I contain the world. I can make of it what I want.' From this Romantic solipsism the anti-vision of the wounded duiker being devoured alive by myriad ants forces him into a new, chastened understanding of 'how things work':

> *It was right* – that was what he was feeling. It was right and nothing could alter it . . .
> . . . The death of that small animal was a thing that concerned him, and he was by no means finished with it. It lay at the back of his mind uncomfortably.
> Soon, the very next morning, he would get clear of everybody and go to the bush and think about it.

Life in the African bush offers this boy with an open, impressionable mind opportunities now almost vanished in the tamed, pastoral landscapes of the Western world, for those moments Wordsworth valued when he recalled:

> Fair seed-time had my soul, and I grew up
> Fostered alike by beauty and by fear.
> $\qquad$ (*The Prelude*, Book I, 301–2)

In several of these stories the child's-eye view yields insight and understandings we come to realize as the potential source of truth which the adult has turned away from (if he ever approached it): '. . . white men coming to Africa take not only what is there, but also impose on it a pattern of their own, from other countries.' ('"Leopard" George')

"Leopard" George, the eccentric but fulfilled possessor of 'bare and bony acres', is of course an exception – though he can only accept the pattern of the place so long as the dark underside does not

---

[1]No page references will be given for quotations from the stories, as there are several editions available: quotations will be attributed in each case to the relevant story.

come too close. The more typical, limited consciousness is a sense of exile, of alienation from the environment and its people except insofar as they can be tamed and turned to use to serve the settler's 'independence', ease or (like the author's father), in a phrase from 'Little Tembi', to fulfil 'vague yearnings towards "freedom"' – most probably from the overcrowded, bureaucratic 'Old Country'. Most simply, Africa is there for use – brutally by a Charlie Slatter (who reappears from *The Grass is Singing* in 'Getting Off the Altitude'), with tidy, decent efficiency by a Major Gale ('The De Wets Come to Kloof Grange') – or a brute fact to be smothered and denied by a more congenial, imposed pattern, as in Mrs. Gale's formal, English garden, or the ill-adjusted modes of living of the successive owners of 'Old John's Place'.

After all, 'This Was the Old Chief's Country' – and will be again. The child's searching eye can go in ignorance behind the imperial arrangements for white settlement to learn the true meaning of 'alienation'. This is most subtly achieved in 'The Old Chief Mshlanga'. Behind this story is the major determining act of white rule in Southern Rhodesia. The Chartered Company that controlled the country till 1923:

> ... [had] pursued the policy of treating the land of Southern Rhodesia as though it had passed entirely out of native ownership and had become the property of the Company's shareholders. It has divided the land into two main categories, 'alienated' and 'unalienated'. Land in the occupancy and ownership of white men is called 'alienated' land. Any native living on 'alienated' land pays the white occupant and owner £1 *per annum*, and a further £1 *per annum* to the Company as head tax. 'Unalienated' land is the land not in the occupancy and ownership of white men, and includes the native 'Reserves'. Natives living in the Reserves pay £1 per head *per annum* to the Company as tax, and another £1 per head for the privilege of living where they do. Portions of this, 'unalienated' land outside the Reserves can, apparently, be taken over at any moment by individual white men, provided, of course, that they obtain the Company's sanction. The natives living on such acquired portions are then expected to pay £1 per head *per annum* to the white acquirer, plus the £1 per head they already pay to the Company.[1]

[1] E. D. Morel, *The Black Man's Burden*, Monthly Review Press, 1969 (first published 1920), p. 49.

Morel was writing before the Government of the country was taken over by the Crown in 1923. However, 'Responsible Government' (as it was termed) did little to remedy these injustices; it was, after all, a settler-dominated government. The Carter Commission, a body set up by the Crown to examine and make recommendations upon the relative needs and rights of the indigenous Africans and the white settlers, gave birth only to the Land Apportionment Act (1930), an Act hardly less odious than the various segregation acts passed in the more overtly discriminatory Union of South Africa:

> The Land Apportionment Act is the basis of Southern Rhodesia policy, as the Group Areas Act is in the Union. In both countries land is parcelled out into areas called Native and European. In Southern Rhodesia only 46 per cent of the land still remains to the Africans. (Whereas in Northern Rhodesia and Nyasaland about 5 per cent has been taken from them.) Since Partnership, this basic segregation has been hardened, not relaxed. Thousands of Africans have been forcibly moved off 'European' land, where they had been living for generations, into Reserves.[1] (The Africans form 95 per cent of the population; thus half the land is held by the white 5 per cent.)

An expert in African history endorses Lessing's view in an amply documented study:

> . . . the Land Apportionment policy hit at all African land interests. People who lived in the Reserves experienced an increasing land shortage and a consequent deterioration of land. Africans who lived in European areas faced eviction without adequate alternatives. Africans who wanted to buy land and set up as progressive farmers were frustrated because much of the Native Purchase land was left unsurveyed and unallocated, largely because of the need to absorb evicted squatters somewhere.[2]

A Shona chief giving evidence before the Carter Commission voiced the common complaint:

> 'When the white man came we thought we were going to be looked after, but it was not so, they have taken land as farms,

---

[1]*Going Home*, op. cit., p. 125.
[2]T. O. Ranger, *The African Voice in Southern Rhodesia 1898–1930* (Heinemann, London, 1970), pp. 227–8.

23

and our sons work for five shillings and then only get a small piece of cloth. We see no prospect of improvement.' 'We were a people who had many cattle, they have all gone. We complained to a people who did not listen.'[1]

These are the pertinent historical facts behind 'The Old Chief Mshlanga'; they are deliberately *kept* behind, the story must make its own unexplained impact:

> Novels, stories, plays, can convey the truth about personal relations, emotions, and attitudes of which the people subject to them are perhaps unaware, or only partly aware: literature comes out of atmospheres, climates of opinion, everything that can not be described by the economic, the sociological approaches.[2]

The purpose of this and other African stories was to convey 'something about what it feels like to live in Rhodesia, and in the South African Republic ... the two countries are similar in atmosphere and political structure. The social conditions out of which they were written exist now.'[2]

Lessing's approach in 'The Old Chief Mshlanga' is through an alien, but not yet alienated consciousness. She takes us first into the fantasy life of a lonely, imaginative white girl. To her the medieval legends of chill Europe are more real than the veld and the African sun; 'the black people on the farm were as remote as the trees and the rocks'. In narrating this story of discovery and revelation Lessing switches from an objective account of what is perhaps a typical child's experience to describe the brash girl's encounter with the courteous old chief in the 'I' form. Living romance enters her life when she realizes 'This Was the Old Chief's Country', but it is hard to fit this knowledge together with the discovery that the chief's son and heir is her father's cook 'boy'. One day she follows beyond the farm's boundaries the path to the Chief's kraal, a path trodden only by Africans (like the boy in 'A Sunrise on the Veld',

---

[1] Ibid., pp. 134–5. It is clear from such evidence as is cited here and elsewhere in Ranger's book that effective power had been in the hands of a settler government prepared to discriminate against the native population, with the passive acquiescence of the Crown, some 40 years before 'U.D.I.' (that government's Unilateral Declaration of Independence from the Crown in 1965).

[2] Author's Introduction to *Nine African Stories*, op. cit., p. 1. While also noting in this Introduction that 'The Old Chief Mshlanga' belongs to the 'thirties, Lessing cites the chief of a tribe faced with dispossession 'fighting in the Courts of Rhodesia to stay on his land' as late as 1967.

discovering Africa where the settler's domain ends). It is a journey into the past of Mashonaland, where she discovers a rooted people living a simple, ancestral life. She asks to see the Chief: 'they did not understand what I wanted. I did not understand myself' – a striking moment of incomprehension. What she does learn is that, in this 'village of ancients and children and women', there is no place for her; one cannot 'dismiss the past with a smile in an easy gush of feeling, saying: I could not help it. I am also a victim.' The serpent of fear and loneliness chills her delight in this paradisal green valley; she is the outcast, she and her race, and that is the deep impression that remains with us despite the sequel when, after a quarrel with her father, the Chief and his kraal are moved to a Reserve two hundred miles away. Their rich land would fall to a new white settler, who would 'wonder what unsuspected vein of richness he had struck' – a vein, we reflect, symbolizing the deprivation of the dispossessed. The sensitive, brooding girl of 'The Old Chief Mshlanga' is of course not typical, which makes her ignorant acceptance of the assumptions of white mastery all the more disturbing: only the 'personal relation' can break this, yet from it must come a nagging consciousness of her inherited guilt for the dispossession. An active concern beyond such fleeting insights is an even rarer life story: this the Martha Quest sequence gives us.

Essential to the success of the short stories in which Africans and native life figure prominently is the author's steady viewpoint. The whites' view, presented usually in the third person but sometimes as a personal anecdote (e.g., 'The Nuisance') is an external one: it can never be their country, though they have tried to take possession of both it and its people. Just as they are always questioning, and often answering their questions too glibly, so the author makes the story itself a query. She is especially interested, not in crass white bigotry, but in the more fruitful themes presented by the failure of the best white efforts to reach the Africans, a failure complemented by the natives' inability or refusal to accept the whites' measure of their mutual relationship. Such stories have an inherent thematic irony which Lessing lets work of itself. Outstanding among them are 'Little Tembi' and 'No Witchcraft for Sale'. The white mistresses in each are enlightened women, up to a point, who strive to establish a personal relation with 'their' natives (the possessive adjective is an ironic element in several stories). In this respect their behaviour is 'Christian': in 'No Witchcraft' Mrs. Farquar's cook is himself a mission 'boy' whose Christian education has taught him the convenient lesson formerly reserved for his counterparts amongst 'lower class' whites; as he and his mistress watch 'a small piccanniny' gazing in wonder at 'the little white boy with his miraculous fair hair and Northern blue eyes':

> The two little children would gaze at each other with a wide, interested gaze, and once Teddy put out his hand curiously to touch the black child's cheeks and hair.
>
> Gideon, who was watching, shook his head wonderingly, and said: 'Ah, missus, these are both children, and one will grow up to be a baas, and one will be a servant'; and Mrs. Farquar smiled and said sadly, 'Yes, Gideon, I was thinking the same.' She sighed. 'It is God's will,' said Gideon, who was a mission boy. The Farquars were very religious people; and this shared feeling about God bound servant and masters even closer together.

The irony of this 'shared feeling' is as grotesque as that of the Victorian domestic servants' acceptance of subservience to their 'betters' (supported by Testamentary texts). 'Love thy neighbour' does not mean accept him as an equal: Mrs. Farquar's warmth toward her cook is self-reflecting: 'she was fond of the old[1] cook because of his love for her child' – one possession serves another. Apparently the cook collaborates in their wishful world until, when the tree-snake spits in the young baas' eye, he goes into his other, African world for the mysterious root that cures. The whites think he will surely reveal to them where that root can be found, so that others may be healed by the black medicine, but he leads them on a futile wild goose chase. It remains Gideon's secret, 'the black man's heritage', *his* possession deeper than any white man's shallow occupation; his is the last, unconsciously ironic word as he looks wistfully at the now grown up white child he saved:

> 'Ah, Little Yellow Head, how you have grown! Soon you will be grown up with a farm of your own . . .'

'Little Tembi' is an ironic exposure of white paternalism in one of its more seductive forms. Jane MacCluster, the nurse who sacrifices her time and energies in a patient, unsentimental way to improve the health and conditions of her husband's workers, surely does as much to pay her moral dues to a subject people as could be expected of anyone – short, that is, of the personal relation. Except

[1]No matter how old, an African servant remains a 'boy'.

in the case of Little Tembi: her mistake is to give him, the pathetic little sufferer, the kind of love she would later give her children, but, after his recovery to withdraw into a normal relationship. Little Tembi's reaction, to try and re-establish the first warm relationship by means that are amusing, then irritating and, finally, estranging – when he turns petty criminal to gain attention – reveals a pathetic, twisted desire *to be possessed*. The MacClusters, only willing to give so much, resort to the pat answer: 'Jane . . . was now feeling that she had "spoiled" Tembi, that he had "got above himself"'. Tembi, for his part, had come to regard himself 'as an apostle of the white man's way of life'. He is a misfit made with the best intentions; the MacClusters can only respond with futile, self-betraying exclamations of incomprehension: 'Tembi behaves as if he had some sort of claim on us', and at the last, when Tembi surrenders himself as passively as Moses in *The Grass is Singing*, to the white man's justice: 'What did he *want*, Willie? What is it he was *wanting*, all this time?' It was nothing they, or anyone in their situation, could have given him; white and black are vexed alike by a thwarted need of true kinship neither can gratify, of which neither is fully aware.[1]

One limit upon her own awareness Lessing scrupulously observes: very rarely does she write from a wholly black viewpoint. One exception is 'The Pig', which evokes the emotions with which a jealous old man kills his young wife's lover with convincing insight and atmospheric evocation of the unnaturalness of the deed in 'a cold moony field' under 'the chilled, moon-green leaves'. This story has a universally intelligible motive; it is a completely plausible reach of the imagination. The normal limits of that reach are provided by an authorial confession of limited knowledge in another story of marital division and, perhaps, murder, 'The Nuisance':

> 'He knows how to handle oxen, but he can't handle his women.'

[1]Nathan M. Shamuyarira (*Crisis in Rhodesia*, Deutsch, London, 1965) is a sensitive, dispassionate analyst of the ambivalent master-servant relationship; he writes: 'The average white farmer is generous and friendly to the untutored African – as long as he accepts his overlordship unquestioningly. Lifetime friendships exist on this pattern; what the Europeans object to is friendship on the basis of equality. An African woman nursemaid, while she is looking after white children, or a driver or waiter can get into any place normally reserved for Europeans, so long as they are doing their job – service. But the moment a driver puts on a tie and jacket and begins to assume some humanity, on his own and separate from the European, then he is not wanted: he is a "cheeky, spoilt native".'

We gave our natives labels such as that, since it was impossible ever to know them as their fellows knew them, in the round.

It is the whites whom we see, and expect to see, 'in the round'. In making this possible Lessing conveys a depth of understanding and insight into white settlerdom far beyond what one might have expected of a writer with her political sympathies. As in *The Grass is Singing* she keeps in view the real humanity of her subjects: few are cut out to be simply oppressors or liberators, self-servers or idealists, in any condition of society. Strands of coarseness and indifference to the suffering of those who are not one's 'own' can lie side by side with a great tenderness and consideration for those one loves, or with a genuine responsibility to those one honestly believes it to be one's duty to govern.

The white men and women of the district of Banket, Lomagundi, of Southern Rhodesia, now Rhodesia, among whom I was brought up, were all good people. That is, they were no better or worse than any handful of white people you could pick out of a crowd. Rather better in many ways, since every one had left a safe and narrow rut of a life out of a sense of adventure and a need to widen horizons, for a country to them wild and often dangerous. It cannot be said that they were a cultivated or wide-minded people, for most fitted Olive Schreiner's description of the South Africans of her time as 'a nation of petty bourgeois philistines'. They still do. But to each other, they were kind, generous, hospitable. . . . At their best, they were (are) not as kind to a black man or a woman as one might be to a dog or a cat.[1]

White itself is a combination of colours. One means of conveying the shades of difference and complexity, as in some of the stories discussed above, is to let them be brought out by the child's freshly observing eye. So in 'Old John's Place' and 'Getting Off the Altitude' that eye searches out the tawdry private life beneath the adult façade of ease and good living; its sensitive search for truth is an acute register of weakness and pathos. More impersonally narrated, 'Lucy Grange' and 'Winter in July' are finely drawn, tense studies of the emotional deprivation borne by the innumerable lonely women sacrificed by their obsessed menfolk to the all absorbing land. This is also, of course, a main theme of *The Grass is*

[1] Doris Lessing, Foreword to L. Vambe, *An Ill-Fated People* (1972), pp. xvi–xvii.

Singing, but in 'Winter in July' Lessing takes her readers into the complex emotional world of three intimately bound people capable of a more subtle, searching response to their existence than the Turners, a world close to that of the Martha Quest sequence. As in that sequence, the woman is the questioner.

'Winter in July' explores the many sides of a tense, triangular relationship between two half-brothers and a woman to whom both are, in effect, married. Tom, the titular husband, is slow, quiet, acceptant; Kenneth quick, evasive, sceptical; Julia, held in 'soft elastic tension' between them, offers them another, less manageable 'country' than that they have made rich. Julia is never at ease in their country, though more sensitive to its manifold meanings than they, seeking to support herself by mental rather than physical knowledge of it. The time comes when the elastic tension gives, and Kenneth resolves to break away and take a wife, to bring a new English woman into this alien setting. The triangle whose shape they have failed to grasp in emotional terms is reduced to a bare geometrical figure beneath the 'arching, myriad-starred, chilly night' of African winter, no more comprehensible than the farm they have long called 'home': 'a large, assertive barn of a place, with its areas of shiny tin roof, the hard pink of the walls, the glinting angled shapes of the windows . . . naked, raw, crude.' Recognizing a crisis but unable to resolve it, Julia turns – as the men have never done – to 'her' country. Yet the land, though she has loved it, can offer no stay in her uncertain middle age for the unsatisfied spirit; that possibility is only perhaps an illusion open to the young:

> She was suffering from an unfamiliar dryness of the senses, an unlocated, unfocused ache that, if she were young, would have formed itself about a person or place, but now remained locked within her. 'What am I?' she kept saying to herself as she walked through the veld, in the moving path of shade that fell from the large drooping hat. On either side the long grass moved and whispered sibilantly; the doves throbbed gently from the trees; the sky was a flower-blue arch over her – it was, as they say, a lovely morning. . . .

> . . . The road back to the house wound along the high hogs'-back between two vleis that fell away on either side. She walked slowly, trying to recover that soft wonder she had felt when she first arrived on the farm and learned how living in cities had cheated her of the knowledge of the shapes of sky and land. Above her, in the great bright bell of blue sky, the

wind currents were marked by swirls of cloud, the backwaters of the air by heavy sculptured piles of sluggish white. Around her the skeleton of rock showed under the thin covering of living soil. The trees thickened with the fall or rise of the ground, with the running of underground rivers; the grass – the long blond hair of the grass – struggled always to heal and hold whatever wounds were made by hoof of beast or thoughtlessness of man. The sky, the land, the swirling air, closed around her in an exchange of water and heat, and the deep multitudinous murmuring of living substance sounded like a humming in her blood. She listened, half-passively, half-rebelliously, and asked: 'What do I contribute to all this?'

That afternoon she walked again, for hours; and throughout the following day; returning to the house punctually for meals, and greeting Tom across the distance that puts itself between people who try to support themselves with the mental knowledge of a country, and those who work in it.

The irony is not only the author's; it underlines the mood and the perception that, of the African, as of the English nature Coleridge celebrated:

> . . . we receive but what we give,
> And in our life alone does Nature live.
>
> ('Dejection: an Ode')

Julia gropes toward the perception the reader has more sharply: 'Look at the way we are – I mean, what do we add up to? What are we doing here, in the first place?' The men laugh at her for developing a political conscience – and she is, but in no conventional sense: she knows that they are living mechanical, ingrown lives, rich and comfortable, but with no meaning outside themselves. There is no resolution, only disenchanted recognition of an unbreakable pattern; Kenneth's young wife imported from England will have to learn, in her turn, to live exiled from more than she will ever find words to express. In 'Winter in July' Africa is, as in all Lessing's African stories, not primarily an arena of racial conflict, but an adaptable setting which she exploits to underline from many sides that alienation – the dryness that cancels the green promise – which all experience but few can voice. 'Julia said slowly and painfully: "I think it is terrible we shouldn't be able to explain what we feel or what we are."'

The characters of 'Winter in July', as in most of the African stories, are white British, but in three of the strongest stories racial and cultural differences between whites dictate the conflicts. These are 'The Second Hut', 'The De Wets Come to Kloof Grange' and 'The Black Madonna'. In the first two it is the traditional antagonism between the English settler and the Afrikaner; the origin of this antagonism lay in the Boer War and the so-called 'century of wrong' that preceded it in South Africa, before the Afrikaners became dominant there only a generation ago – in a land where they saw themselves as pioneers and rightful first claimants. That antagonism is not Lessing's main theme (she takes it as understood), just as in the stories previously discussed she is not concerned solely with the colour conflict. Going to the heart of the matter, she depicts instead the fumbling, pathetic individual lives of a people who, however vehemently they seek to claim Africa as their own, will remain forever alien.

In 'The Second Hut' her interest is again in those on the border of failure: Major Carruthers, 'a gentleman farmer going to seed', his wife heartbroken 'over the conditions they lived in', the Afrikaans assistant, Van Heerden, down on his luck and obliged to engage himself to a 'traditional enemy'. The story ironically turns upon racial distinctions cut even finer than the Major is aware of. The dilapidated hut is the only accommodation he will offer Van Heerden, since he will not offer so uncouth a being 'a corner in his house' (as he would willingly have done for a fellow Englishman), yet he frets under a hardened feeling, caused by 'his being responsible for another human being having to suffer such conditions'. (Between the lines read for 'another human being' 'a *white* man'.) When he makes the worse discovery that Van Heerden is not, as he had been led to believe, a single man, but that he has a wife and nine children the Major's worst fears have come alive:

> Fear rose high in him. For a few moments he inhabited the landscape of his dreams, a grey country full of sucking menace, where he suffered what he would not allow himself to think of while awake: the grim poverty that could overtake him if his luck did not turn, and if he refused to submit to his brother and return to England.
>
> Walking through the fields, where the maize was now waving over his head, pale gold with a froth of white, the sharp dead leaves scything crisply against the wind, he could see nothing but that black foetid hut and the pathetic futureless

children. That was the lowest he could bring his own children to! He felt moorless, helpless, afraid: his sweat ran cold on him. And he did not hesitate in his mind; driven by fear and anger, he told himself to be hard; he was searching in his mind for the words with which he would dismiss the Dutch man who had brought his worst nightmares to life, on his own farm, in glaring daylight, where they were inescapable.

Not simply guilt, but a desire to erect a bulwark, however frail, against the slide into poverty he foresees for his own family, causes the Major to decide to provide the Van Heerdens with a second hut. The unforeseen clash this brings with his hitherto pliable workers, who loathe Van Heerden for brutal slave-driving, but must build that hut, is a form of rough, ironic justice. The Major is entangled in a web of 'fine feelings': the codes of the English 'gentleman', the white man in exile, the paternal master will not mix. Van Heerden has committed the white's unforgivable sin of 'going native', which really means slipping into the poverty endured by the native. A poverty, and this is another irony, not felt by the Major to be attuned to African nature beneath 'the wide hall of fresh blue sky':

> The beautiful clear weather that he usually loved so much, May weather, sharpened by cold, and crisp under deep clear skies, pungent with gusts of wind from the dying leaves and grasses of the veld, was spoilt for him this year: something was going to happen.

Yet Van Heerden's reaction after the burning of the hut, presumably by a resentful African, and the death of a child, shows him to be not only in tune with the harsh demands of a native life but capable of a tender, albeit rough concern for his wife and children akin in a positive sense to that of the beast the Major has taken him for. It is this revelation that defeats the Major and shows his and his fretful wife's unfitness for a life they have chosen with so faint a heart.

Again, as in 'Winter in July', the woman, the Major's wife – though more in the background – is the vessel of discontent. Mrs. Carruthers takes to her bed; in 'The De Wets Come to Kloof Grange' Major Gale's wife is in a material position to build a more restful retreat, a little England in Africa in the shape of her eighteenth-century English room and two acres of tamed garden: 'she has learned to love her isolation'. Into this intrudes the new Afrikaans overseer's young wife, Betty, bringing with her an untamed passion and restlessness Mrs. Gale has put behind her. Betty is drawn beyond the garden to the 'green-crowded gully' with its 'intoxicating heady smell'[1] : these Mrs. Gale has come to ignore, setting her gaze on '*her* hills' beyond, but to the brash girl it is 'a lovely smell' and she goes off into the bush to commune with it rather than bow to Mrs. Gale's stilted companionship. Similarly Van Heerden's fecund wife finds content in her drowse of children, seeming to the Major's fastidious eyes 'less a human being than an elemental, irrepressible force': thus these two unsophisticated women collaborate instinctively with 'Africa' while the finer whites shrink into attenuated cultivated patches of it. Mrs. Gale glimpses this insight when, after Betty has pretended to run away, she 'hated her garden, that highly-cultivated patch of luxuriant growth, stuck in the middle of a country that could do this sort of thing to you so suddenly' – but when she learns the girl's flight was a stratagem to regain her husband's attention and love she withdraws from her insight and labels it 'savage'.

'The Black Madonna' introduces an alien element unique among these stories, an element fortuitously provided by the conditions of the Second World War. It is, Lessing wrote recently, 'full of the bile that is produced in me by the thought of "white" society in Southern Rhodesia as I knew and hated it.'[2] It was placed first in the original collection, *African Stories*, its opening paragraphs like a crude signpost: 'Zambesia is a tough, sunburnt, virile, positive country contemptuous of subtleties and sensibility . . .' Though there is much in this unusually hard-edged satirical vein in the opening paragraphs, the story modulates in its portrayal of the Captain into one of Lessing's most compassionate studies of a sensibility violated by an inhuman code of behaviour. The Captain's antagonist, the simple Italian artist Michele, exposes the want of 'heart' which makes and keeps the country what it is: for Michele, it is a plain truth that the Madonna he paints for the church should be black, 'Black peasant Madonna for black country'. To the Captain, this is an impossible heresy: 'You can't have a black Madonna', he protests: for him there is no contradiction in the assumption that you *can* have a black mistress, his 'bushwife' Nadya – though only in one capacity. Sacred is White; profane Black. Under the skin the Captain senses the warping limitations of this, in human as in spiritual love, but he

[1] The setting that creates the contrast between 'Nature methodiz'd' and nature untamed is reminiscent of Coleridge's 'Kubla Khan'.
[2] Preface to *The Sun Beneath Their Feet*, op. cit., p. 9.

must repress it to keep his universe in order. The picture is to be blown up anyway as part of the model village the Army has erected for an artillery demonstration, but its very existence is the explosive seed that mines the too rigid structure of the Captain's personality. At the end, as he lies in hospital convalescing after what his superiors see as one of those strange disintegrations white men suffer in these taxing climes, Michele comes offering what he naïvely supposes will be a more acceptable picture – of a halo-*less* black girl. The Captain refuses it with indignation, but, after the white-haired Italian has left, turns his face to the wall and weeps – silently, 'for the fear the nurses might hear'. This story is inescapably reminiscent of the way E. M. Forster uses Italians in his early novels and stories as a foil to the repressed English; also, of how in English rule in the imperial situation of *A Passage to India* the tragic lack is 'one touch of the heart'. Both writers, at separate times and places, bring out with sadness more than anger how the need of a superior race to maintain an impregnable front before 'the lesser breeds', the male driver needed to 'tame' or run the land, must poison the personal life at its source.

It is worth noting that, though this affinity between Forster and Lessing is clear, it is rather one of feeling than style: Lessing is more prepared than he to let situation and character speak for itself and eschews the explicit authorial comment that draws out themes and conflicts in such terms as 'heart' and 'head', 'inner' and 'outer' (life), 'prose' and 'passion'. Her affinity with D. H. Lawrence, as a delineator of involved emotional relationships whose meaning defies clear categorization, is stronger – though again, she is less liable than he to authorial pointing either through overt comment or heavily expressive symbolism. An especially notable affinity is their characterization of women as the sensitive receivers and moulders of experience, the potential agents of change.[1] In the stories discussed in this chapter, because the author is portraying an ingrown, self-limiting society, these tendencies are thwarted, stunted, impotent: that society's exceptional woman, who takes the initiative towards thought *and* carries it through, is reserved for the ampler scope of the Martha Quest novels.

---

[1] Some critics have claimed that Lessing's early work must have been influenced by Lawrence, but I can see no justification for going beyond *affinities*: the elements of action, plot, characterization and setting stem naturally from her subject matter: clearer evidence of influence would be in language and imagery, but there are no substantial links in these respects.

4   The Short Novels

Of the four African novels first published in the collection entitled *Five* in 1953, three are among her finest works, while the fourth, 'Hunger', is her weakest and least characteristic. Nevertheless, the collection was awarded the Somerset Maugham prize, for the best work of the year by an English author under thirty-five, in 1954.

These short novels fall between short story length and that even of the usual short novel. They can best be distinguished from the short stories proper in Lessing's own words: 'There is space in them to take one's time, to think aloud, to follow, for a paragraph or two, on a side-trail – none of which is possible in a real short story.'[1] There are risks as well as advantages in this looser method, which the failure of 'Hunger' illustrates; the risks are greater when the story's message is uppermost in the author's mind, as she has admitted it was:

2068557

> It came to be written like this. I was in Moscow with a delegation of writers, back in 1952. It was striking that while the members of the British team differed very much politically, we agreed with each other on certain assumptions about literature – in brief, that writing had to be a product of the individual conscience, or soul. Whereas the Russians did not agree at all – not at all. Our debates, many and long, were on this theme.
>
> Stalin was still alive. One day we were taken to see a building full of presents for Stalin, rooms full of every kind of object – pictures, photographs, carpets, clothes, etc., all gifts from his grateful subjects and exhibited by the State to show other subjects and visitors from abroad. It was a hot day. I left the others touring the stuffy building and sat outside to rest. I

[1] Preface to *African Stories* (1964), reprinted in *Collected African Stories*, Volume One, p. 8.

was thinking about what Russians were demanding in literature – greater simplicity, simple judgments of right and wrong. We, the British, had argued against it, and we felt we were *right* and the Russians *wrong*. But after all, there was Dickens, and such a short time ago, and his characters were all good or bad – unbelievably Good, monstrously Bad, but that didn't stop him from being a great writer. Well, there I was, with my years in Southern Africa behind me, a society as startlingly unjust as Dickens's England. Why, then, could I not write a story of simple good and bad, with clear-cut choices, set in Africa? The plot? Only one possible plot – that a poor black boy or girl should come from a village to the white man's rich town and . . . there he would encounter, as occurs in life, good and bad, and after much trouble and many tears he would follow the path of . . .

I tried, but it failed. It wasn't true. Sometimes one writes things that don't come off, and feels more affectionate towards them than towards those that worked.[1]

Lessing's affection for 'Hunger' is easy to understand, for its failure is one of good intentions, of an anxiety that the message be conveyed overmastering the story-telling function. Plot and viewpoint were inevitably major problems. 'Hunger' has one of the 'basic plots' amongst those earliest established in South African writing[2] and long before that, as her reference to Dickens indicates, in the early Victorian English novels intended to reveal the life of the underworld. Jabavu runs through a fairly predictable gamut of experiences; as Mr. Samu, the African politician who befriends him, is made to comment: 'His experiences are typical for young men coming to town.'[3] Jabavu's very name is symbolic. White City Jabavu is the name of one of the suburbs of Soweto (South Western Township), the agglomeration of dormitory suburbs attached to Johannesburg; of this a Black African poet, Oswald Mtshali, has written:

> I don't see
> anything white
> in this White City –

[1] Preface to *Collected African Stories*, Volume Two, p. 8.
[2] E.g., R. R. R. Dhlomo's *An African Tragedy* (1928). 'Basic plots' is Lessing's phrase: 'this is the story of the African in modern Africa' (*Going Home*, op. cit., p. 163).
[3] *Five* (Penguin edition, 1960), p. 313.

just the blackness
of widow's garments
of mourning.[1]

The town of the story is of course not Johannesburg, but that most seductive of all traps for the 'bush' African is often mentioned in the story and supplies, as it were, the prototype of all 'Joe Comes to Jo'burg' stories.

To the reader unfamiliar with the pattern such stories had taken for some forty years 'Hunger' will at least be fresh in subject matter. If he comes to it with a grounding in English literature he will notice rather, in Jabavu's initiation into the life of the 'skellums' ('wicked persons') in the city – his instruction in petty thievery, his urge to goodness though he does wrong – and in the characterization of the prostitute, Betty, and the gang-leader Jerry, strong resemblances to *Oliver Twist*. These are in plot and a tendency to enforce the theme with black and white oppositions. Beyond these, there are touches of characterization that have possibilities of depth for which the story allows no scope, as for example in the analysis of Betty whose 'nature' it is 'to love the indifference of man'.[2]

The difficulty of striking an apt viewpoint is evident from the very beginning. Stopping short of adopting a completely 'inside' presentation of Jabavu, which might have seemed to claim too much, the narrator becomes a camera eye, seeing him from the outside, alternating with a recording voice that witnesses thoughts and feelings. The immediate effect is to give the reader a disturbingly objective view of character and situation, as of a documentary about a strange people. The explanatory comment, on the degradation of life in the kraal, the childlike 'hunger' of the young for 'the white man's town', the heavy despair of the old at the passing of the traditional way of life and its corruption by the new, increase the distancing effect of the narration in the present tense. In large part the author's problem is that she cannot assume in her reader enough vital knowledge, but the effect is more damaging when her characters become mere mouthpieces for representative attitudes than when the narrative smoothly supplies this kind of ironical touch on Jabavu's physical examination at the Pass Office:

> The doctor has said, too, that Jabavu has an enlarged spleen, which means he has had malaria and will have it again,

---

[1] 'White City Jabavu', *Sounds of a Cowhide Drum* (O.U.P., London, 1971), p. 52.
[2] *Five*, op. cit., p. 304.

that he probably has bilharzia, and there is a suspicion of hookworm. But these are too common for comment, and what the doctor is looking for are diseases which may infect the white people if he works in their houses.[1]

Perhaps because there is so much ammunition in the story that may be used against white rule and for African solidarity it has been, as Lessing thinks, one of her 'most liked' despite, or because of, its artistic simplification. Morality tales have always had their appeal, and are in fact the stuff of officially approved 'literature' in modern Russia and China. We should remember that 'Hunger' was written when Lessing had returned flushed with political purpose from Moscow: no other story from her Communist years has so markedly political a flavour. The last page, when the imprisoned Jabavu becomes fired with a revived sense of the old tribal solidarity after reading the letter from the African leader, Mr. Mizi, could with little difficulty be converted into a paean prophesying the ultimate victory of the workers: '*We*, says Jabavu over and over again, *We*. And it is as if in his empty hands are the warm hands of brothers.' It is surely no accident that the fact that it is Mr. Mizi's message which touches Jabavu, not Mr. Tennent's, 'the man of God' – to whom Mizi is 'an intemperate and godless agitator' – contrasts so sharply with the Christian answer that closes Alan Paton's *Cry, the Beloved Country*. Our belief in Jabavu's ability to absorb Mr. Mizi's message strains to the utmost the author's need throughout to make us accept him as an exceptionally clever, almost entirely self-taught literate. In order to convey the message Jabavu has to carry too large a burden of probability, as did the working-class heroes of the Victorian novel-with-a-purpose or of Communist proletarian literature today. It is as well that Lessing only had one such lapse, but valuable that we have it still as a cautionary tale.[2]

Turning to 'The Antheap', we find the problems of articulating complex feeling and of avoiding excessive commentary admirably solved. All grows naturally out of close relationship between the three principal actors: old Mr. Macintosh, the millionaire

---

[1] Ibid., p. 282.
[2] The endings of 'Little Tembi' and *The Grass is Singing* have a more satisfying openness. Cf. also the sure handling of the short dramatic episode about Jabavu's poor white counterparts, 'A Road to the Big City' (*African Stories*).

goldminer, his unwanted half-caste son Dirk, and Dirk's white friend Tommy Clarke, Macintosh's engineer's son whom he loves as if he were his own. The problem of communication between these three, who are repeatedly barred from mutual understanding by conflicting emotions that run deep and strong, and by sheer incapacity to enter fully into the thoughts and feelings of the others, is solved (as in 'The Black Madonna') by the casting of Tommy as artist. His art expresses more than he can say or consciously know: it communicates this knowledge to the others who, like him, are locked in pride, hatred and distrust. This means of communication is, of course, one that comes most naturally to the author; it enables her to convey the deeper meaning with a rich suggestiveness.

As in some of the short stories, the adoption of the child's eye view allows freshness of vision and response to a situation the adult characters have come to regard with a stale, hardened acceptance. It is natural that Tommy Clarke, the solitary white boy, should turn to the nearest children for playmates even though they are 'kaffirs'.[1] It is natural, too, that the one to whom he feels closest should be the half-caste Dirk, the boss's unacknowledged son; wanted by neither black nor white, the 'coloured' is the one against whom the barrier of 'silence' and segregation is strongest. This very difficulty naturally spurs Tommy's attempts to breach it, rather than any precocious instinct for equality – that comes later, after the personal relationship has been established. When he asks his parents, 'Why shouldn't I play with Mr. Macintosh's son?' he is using the system, not revolting against it. The story never drops, throughout the slow progress of the relationship and of Tommy's insight, into simple heroics. With great wisdom Lessing analyses the feeling that holds the two boys, supplying the perception of what Tommy only dimly comprehends:

> What, then, was friendship? Dirk was his friend, that he knew, but did he like Dirk? Did he love him? Sometimes not at all. He remembered how Dirk had said: 'I'll get you another baby buck. I'll kill its mother with a stone.' He remembered his feeling of revulsion at the cruelty. Dirk was cruel. But – and here Tommy unexpectedly laughed, and for the first time he understood Dirk's way of laughing. It was

[1]'kaffir . . . must be accepted as meaning simply a dark-skinned inhabitant of South Africa who is not descended from Bushmen or Hottentots or Asiatics, and is not a mixture of brown and white breeds. It is as general a term as that.' (Sarah Gertrude Millin, *The South Africans*, London: Constable, 2nd Edition, 1934, p. 24.)

really funny to say that Dirk was cruel, when his very existence was a cruelty. Yet Mr. Macintosh laughed in exactly the same way, and his skin was white, or rather, white browned over by the sun. Why was Mr. Macintosh also entitled to laugh, with that same abrupt ugliness? Perhaps somewhere in the beginnings of the rich Mr. Macintosh there had been the same cruelty, and that had worked its way through the life of Mr. Macintosh until it turned into the cruelty of Dirk, the coloured boy, the half-caste? If so, it was all much deeper than differently coloured skins, and much harder to understand.

And then Tommy thought how Dirk seemed to wait always, as if he, Tommy, were bound to stand by him, as if this were a justice that was perfectly clear to Dirk; and he, Tommy, did in fact fight with Mr. Macintosh for Dirk, and he could behave in no other way. Why? Because Dirk was his friend? Yet there were times when he hated Dirk, and certainly Dirk hated him, and when they fought they could have killed each other easily, and with joy.

Well, then? Well, then? What was friendship, and why were they bound so closely, and by what? Slowly the little boy, sitting alone on his antheap came to an understanding which is proper to middle-aged people, that resignation in knowledge which is called irony. Such a person may know, for instance, that he is bound most deeply to another person, although he does not like that person, in the way the word is ordinarily used, or like the way he talks, or his politics, or anything else. And yet they are friends and will always be friends, and what happens to this bound couple affects each most deeply, even though they may be in different continents, or may never seen each other again. Or after twenty years they may meet, and there is no need to say a word, everything is understood. This is one of the ways of friendship, and just as real as amiability or being alike.

Well, then? For it is a hard and difficult knowledge for any little boy to accept. But he accepted it, and knew that he and Dirk were closer than brothers and always would be so.[1]

This brotherhood, unlike that too easily invoked in 'Hunger', is literally fought for with what continues to the end to be an almost desperate urge toward fulfilment. When Macintosh gives in and

[1] *Five*, op. cit., p. 205.

40

concedes chances of education to both boys, making them as equal at least as their society will allow, a new phase in their lives inevitably begins, to surmount the barrier that may yet break them; it remains an open question whether they can or will:

> The victory was entirely theirs, but now they had to begin again, in the long and difficult struggle to understand what they had won and how they would use it.[1]

Only in this last sentence does the novel take the clearer-cut form of a parable and do we suddenly see the boys as more than themselves, as the symbols of promise for the future – or failure. Thus, the method reverses the approach in 'Hunger', where the symbolic overtones are insistently present from the outset. The essential separateness of all, white and black, it is borne in upon us, is underlined by Dirk's special role of outcast: though he is the child of both races, he is accepted by neither.

Tommy Clarke, the sensitive white boy, could easily have become sentimentalized. Instead of *using* him for the facile purpose of demonstrating the superiority of his perceptions to adult prejudice, Lessing lets him be drawn to Dirk by a complex of motives: the desire for companionship, the need to assert his wishes against the prohibitions of his parents, a fascinated compulsion to play with his 'superiority', the little-understood urges of his artistic self. From the moment he moulds a rough clay image of Dirk he becomes the agent of intuitive meaning: that first image is also the first constructive use of that African earth which Mr. Macintosh has obsessively pillaged, his carving of Dirk's mother and child stirs in Mr. Macintosh inexpressible feelings of bafflement and loss, the frieze of the mine becomes the pit of hell. Tommy carves, not only what he sees, but what he half knows: this Mr. Macintosh acknowledges, struggling between his love for the boy and fear of his art, in the only way he and his kind have ever known. He buys the advice of the art expert Mr. Tomlinson, who tells him of Tommy's second carving of Dirk, in a moment of ironic comedy: 'It has a look of you' . . . The ironies accumulate: Macintosh's money, wrenched from the African earth, becomes the means of 'investing' in Tommy's talent, though that is itself both a reverent, creative use of that earth and a challenge to the social subjection the 'antheap' symbolizes:

> Dirk was looking at himself. 'Why do you make me like

[1] *Five*, op. cit., p. 237.

that?' he asked. The narrow, strong face expressed nothing but that familiar, sardonic antagonism, as if he said: 'You, too – just like the rest!'

'Why? Why don't you like it?' challenged Tommy at once.

Dirk walked around it, then back. 'You're just like all the rest,' he said.

'Why? Why don't you like it?' Tommy was really distressed. Also, his feeling was: What's it got to do with him? Slowly he understood that his emotion was that belief in his right to freedom which Dirk always felt immediately, and he said in a different voice: 'Tell me what's wrong with it?'

'Why do I have to come out of the wood? Why haven't I any hands or feet?'

'You have, but don't you see . . .' But Tommy looked at Dirk standing in front of him and suddenly gave an impatient movement: 'Well, it doesn't matter, it's only a statue.'

He sat on the trunk and Dirk beside him. After a while he said: 'How should you be, then?'

'If you make yourself, would you be half wood?'

Tommy made an effort to feel this, but failed. 'But it's not me, it's you.' He spoke with difficulty, and thought: But it's important, I shall have to think about it later. He almost groaned with the knowledge that here it was, the first debt, presented for payment.

Dirk said suddenly: 'Surely it needn't be wood. You could do the same thing if you put handcuffs on my wrists.' Tommy lifted his head and gave a short, astonished laugh. 'Well, what's funny?' said Dirk, aggressively. 'You can't do it the easy way, you have to make me half wood, as if I was more a tree than a human being.'

Tommy laughed again, but unhappily. 'Oh, I'll do it again,' he acknowledged at last. 'Don't fuss about that one, it's finished. I'll do another.'

There was silence.[1]

Both understand more than they can say: as at the beginning of their relationship, when the boy Tommy had troubled his parents by '[infringing] the rule of silence'[2] linked with Dirk, so at the end. This 'silence' cannot be bridged by slogans or wishful attitudes; it is an inescapable condition of their existence.

[1] Ibid., pp. 234–5.
[2] Ibid., p. 194.

In 'Eldorado', as in 'The Antheap', the elusive private worlds of emotion and desire of a closely-knit trio who can never be at one are again held in uneasy relationship by a potent symbolic force. This is the lure of gold – a dream, 'gleam', vision or trap, destroyer of sanity even; it is like the compulsion of art, its own reward or damnation, depending on your point of view. Yet it is a symptom, not a cause. The old wandering prospector who comes to the Barnes' farm and who 'spoke of the search for gold as a scientist might of a discovery, or an artist of his art'[1] is no devil, leading Alec Barnes astray from the straight, if unspectacular path of farming maize. He is one visionary speaking to another, soul to soul. The search for gold that draws Alec into neglect of his farm only gives a new impetus to that need for 'freedom', that instinct for 'distance', an unconfined world all his own making, which first brought Alec out to the colony. His wife recognizes it with dread, her love cannot reach it.

> That *something else* – how well Maggie knew it! And how she grieved for Paul, whose heart was beating (she could positively hear it) to the pulse of that dangerous *something else*. It was not the elephants and the lions and the narrow escapes; not the gold; not underground rivers; none of these things in themselves, and perhaps not even the pursuit of them. It was that oblique, unnamable quality in life which Maggie, trying to pin it down safely in homely words, finally dismissed in the sour and nagging phrase: Getting something for nothing.[2]

She tries to warn her son Paul against this lure. Of course, he does not understand. Like so many of Lessing's children, he oscillates uneasily between his parents' two worlds, condemned by love, shame, antagonism and the sheer necessity of close relationship to seek his own standing point apart from both.

'Eldorado' is one of Lessing's most painful treatments of a family relationship. Of how the bonds of blood and natural dependence war against the 'free' self-realization that each desires. Opposed to the father's self-centred vision of 'freedom' is that which the mother desires for her son: 'Knowledge freed a man; and to that belief she clung, because it was her nature; and she was to grieve all her life because such a simple and obvious truth was not simple for Paul.'[3] Knowing he hasn't the academic ability, and looking for a

---

[1] *Five*, op. cit., p. 134.
[2] Ibid., p. 142.
[3] Ibid., p. 161.

solid form of security in reaction from his father's failure and drift into a world of fantasy, Paul turns to James, the rough and ready 'small-worker' whose mine lies on the farm's boundary. James is a drunkard, sleeps with native women – a minor version of Macintosh – is grounded in a saving earthy realism. Throwing in his lot with James, Paul fulfils Maggie's worst fears, that he would 'grow up lax and happy-go-lucky, like a Colonial'.[1] Her husband and son combine in this, that they bear out her conviction – felt by so many of Lessing's women but rarely voiced – that 'the very country was against her'.[2] The woman, with her dreams of order, security, a civilized life, knows that her unbeatable antagonist is Africa: Africa rude, vital, capricious, is the 'Other Woman' she must fear; her men will loot it, love it, rape it or be seduced by it away from her. To it, in 'Eldorado', Maggie loses both her men: Paul, the son, will loot that earth; her husband Alec scarcely sane at the last, will be bound for the rest of his life to its charms. Faithful to the gold that eludes him (but gives itself, indifferently, to his son), it is enough for him that it exists: '. . . all he said was, and in a proud, pleased voice: "Well, that proves it. I told you, didn't I? I always told you so."'[3]

So human loves are lost to the seductive earth. These three can only talk with their feeling eyes, watchful, dark, evasive, full of pain. They tremble often upon the verge of loving connection, of pity given and accepted, but always their natures drive them apart. Mrs. Barnes blames the country, but she is as wrong as those characters of Hardy's who rail against adverse 'Nature'; only in countries of the mind is happiness attainable, and this ironically is Alec's one treasure – 'safe in that orderly inner world he had built for himself'.[4]

Of the stories so far discussed in this and the previous chapter, those centring upon the white settlers and their lives deal with what may be called the 'true' settler's life: the principal antagonist is the African earth, a secondary one can be the recalcitrant native. The situation is long-established and its main lines understood by white and black alike; occasionally one or the other oversteps the bounds, as happens in 'Little Tembi', a few have restless stirrings toward

[1] Ibid., p. 129.
[2] Ibid., p. 128.
[3] Ibid., p. 179.
[4] Ibid., p. 160.

something better, like Julia in 'Winter in July', but on the whole their conservative rural society keeps such spirits within conforming limits. Members of both races, whether it be Jabavu's father in 'Hunger' or Maggie Barnes in 'Eldorado', fear and distrust the city, which is synonymous with social disorder and the confusion of values. (The irony remains, of course, that the orders and values of the 'country' are those imposed by the white man for his own convenience.) This contrast and conflict between a stable rural and a corrupt urban life is, of course, one of the oldest themes in literature. In the Rhodesian, or any similar Colonial situation, only in the very few major cities is there any possibility of access to the values of a more open society. Into such towns there has over the past thirty or forty years been a steady flow of potentially disruptive influences – whites who have no stake in the 'country', but come to work often only for a few years in the schools, universities, the Civil Service or the developing industrial concerns. (We shall see how a large part of the Martha Quest sequence turns to portraying such people.) However, it must be remembered that while these newer colonials may be the bearers of more enlightened ideas, they nevertheless have hardly less interest than the rural settler in maintaining their ascendancy over the blacks. A piquant irony is inherent in this contradiction, which Lessing exploits to the full in 'A Home for the Highland Cattle', a masterpiece of ironic comedy.

Ironies multiply from the outset. We are going to read of a new type of white emigrant:

> It seems, from books, that the colonizers and adventurers went sailing off to a new fine life, a new country, opportunities, and so forth. Now all they want is a roof over their heads.[1]

This sets the deflating tone of the whole story. The town (Salisbury) to which the Gileses come was to have been the bold city of Cecil Rhodes' vision; actually, it is the mean suburban world of the 'Old Country' transplanted to an 'exotic' setting inhabited by ten thousand whites and serviced by 150,000 blacks who 'do not so much *live* here, as squeeze themselves in as they can'.[2] It soon dawns upon Marina Giles, who had come out as 'that liberally-minded person produced so plentifully in England during the thirties', that her vision was no less fatuous than Rhodes's:

---

[1] *Five*, p. 9.
[2] Ibid., p. 10.

... what is a British Colony but a sort of highly-flavoured suburb of England itself? Somewhere in the back of Marina's mind has been a vision of herself and Philip living in a group of amiable people, pleasantly interested in the arts, who read the *New Statesman* week by week, and held that discreditable phenomena like the colour bar and the black-white struggle could be solved by sufficient goodwill ... a delightful picture.[1]

Life's necessities bring Marina's concerns down to a depressingly humdrum level. Like countless colonial wives before her, she is confounded by the 'servant problem' – reviving that very problem of conscience and convenience which good liberals in the 'Old Country' had disposed of a generation earlier. Ironically, it is one which their modern descendants now go abroad to encounter all over again. Throughout the colonial period it was inevitably the woman's problem, so that in India the '*memsahib*', in Africa the 'madam' found herself at the most sensitive point of contact with the native. We have seen the tragic side of this in *The Grass is Singing*: 'A Home for the Highland Cattle' exploits its more comic possibilities, though the effects are nonetheless serious.

While Philip, her agriculturist husband, devotes his energies to furthering the African's well-being in his practical, worthwhile way, Marina struggles in their semi-detached box, 138 Cecil Rhodes Vista (wicked name!) to realize her notions of human equality in her handling of her 'boy', Charlie. From the beginning Charlie gropes to comprehend this new variety of 'madam' and clearly it will not be long before, as most servants will, he takes advantage of her guilt-ridden weakness.

This story requires a comic symbol. Nothing could have been more apt than one of those Victorian pictures of highland cattle, which used to be endemic in 'Old Country' drawing rooms and parlours ('Really, why bother to emigrate?'[2]). Mrs. Skinner, the landlady, leaves it to Marina's safe-keeping. Marina, naturally, abhors it: it is the persistent image of what she had intended to escape. Charlie, however, seems to admire it – an admiration dimly connected, she supposes, with the part played by cattle in tribal life

[1] Ibid., p. 13. (The *New Statesman* has been since the thirties the most widely read moderate Left weekly in England: D.L. herself contributed several reviews and articles to it during the fifties; it is the *New Statesman* that arouses Martha's liberal conscience in *Martha Quest*.)
[2] Ibid., p. 19.

'that could only be described as religious'.[1] This part is the use of cattle as *lobola* (the 'bride-price' paid by the suitor to his loved one's father), now in a sadly degenerated state.[2] Gradually, Marina works herself into a false position: her attempts to treat Charlie more humanely 'spoil' him, as Little Tembi was spoiled by Jane MacCluster; she becomes so embroiled in his personal life that she falls ironically into the despised role of the white paternalist, handling her Africans as foolish children. Her attempt to get Charlie married to Theresa, his pregnant girl-friend, brings the picture into play. Thinking it valuable, Charlie has the bright idea of presenting it to Theresa's father in lieu of *lobola*; and Marina, compromising her white integrity, agrees to give it him. She and Philip drive the pair and the picture out to the wretched location where the father exists, only to receive from the broken old man a nostalgic homily on the degenerate state into which the old ritual and ceremonies have fallen. Nevertheless, he accepts the picture. Philip and Marina drive back, grim but little wiser, unknowingly leaving the couple to celebrate their union in an illicit liquor den. The sequel is no less sordid. When Mrs. Skinner gets an inkling upon her return of what those 'white kaffirs' (the Gileses) have done with her precious painting, she has no difficulty in getting Charlie arrested for carrying off a few worthless objects including 'a wooden door-knocker that said '*Welcome Friend*'.[3]

The sequel is crisp and could stand as epitaph for a legion of good intentions, fatally unsupported by imagination, like Marina's. Marina, having at last graduated into the higher suburbs she had at first scorned and ignorant of Charlie's fate, passes a file of handcuffed prisoners in a street 'in this city of what used to be known as the Dark Continent',[4] thinks momentarily that she recognizes Charlie among them but, intent on discovering that 'ideal table' at once dismisses the thought. Her well-intentioned but amateurish meddling has merely violated the accepted order of

[1] Ibid., p. 35.
[2] Due to the Government's scheme for 'destocking' of cattle: 'Africans were told to reduce the number of their cattle to a maximum of five; though designed for the sake of good husbandry, it removed 'the cornerstone of African marriage and laws. . . . The normal exchange of ten head of cattle, from the son-in-law to his father-in-law, was made impossible . . . the *lobola* of cattle provided the only tangible bond of the new union between two families.' (Shamuyarira, op. cit., p. 96.)
[3] Ibid., p. 61.
[4] Ibid., p. 62.

things, causing both Charlie's misfortune (though he endures it with a well-taught philosophy) and her tired indifference. By now the story could be sub-titled 'The Making of a Madam'. We should not overlook in these closing paragraphs the significance of the reference to the Dark Continent in juxtaposition with the file of handcuffed prisoners: it ironically suggests the slave caravans of the days before white enlightenment. . . . In 'A Home for the Highland Cattle', exercising a firm, ironic control as assured as Forster's in *A Passage to India*, Lessing has, like that pioneering ironist of the diseased heart of imperialism, subtly exposed the perils of liberal efforts at 'connexion', if unsupported by extraordinary character and intelligence.[1] It is a cautionary tale whose meaning can be applied to many situations other than the one that directly inspired it: claims to enlightened attitudes are far more easily professed than lived up to.

[1] The story's impact, as I have suggested, sharpens the 'idea' that Lessing tells us she began with: ' "A Home for the Highland Cattle" I wrote after watching a charming, liberal lady, newly immigrant to Rhodesia, who hated the society she found herself in – but eventually succumbed. She was not strong enough to fight it.' (*Nine African Stories*, op. cit., p. 8.)

5 Children of Violence: Form and Purpose

In every period of literature there are created figures whom readers at once recognize as figures of their age, in whom they may see reflected their own situation, circumstances, desires, illusions and disillusions. Particularly has this been so during the past two hundred years with the slackening of the hold that religion in the West formerly had upon the ordinary person's conscience and imagination. The heroine of 'Children of Violence', Martha Quest, herself such a figure, has been similarly influenced:

> . . . she was of that generation who, having found nothing in religion, had formed themselves by literature. And the books which spoke most directly were those which had come out of Western Europe during the past hundred years, and of those, the personal and self-confessing . . . for it is a remarkable fact that she was left unmoved by criticisms of the sort of person she was by parents, relations, preachers, teachers, politicians and people who write for the newspapers; whereas an unsympathetic description of a character similar to her own in a novel would send her into a condition of anxious soul-searching for days.[1]

The literary figures who serve for readers as a measure of their own lives are, of course, as diverse as the nature of individuality, but they have one common characteristic: they are conscious as individuals of being divorced from their society and its ruling assumptions – whether they be Goethe's Werther, Byron's Childe Harold, Charlotte Brontë's Jane Eyre, Flaubert's Emma Bovary, Raskolnikov in Dostoievsky's *Crime and Punishment*, Lyndall in *The Story of an African Farm* or in *Sons and Lovers* D. H. Lawrence's Paul Morel. (This is a random sampling from a much larger company,

---

[1] *A Proper Marriage* (Panther edition, London, 1966), p. 73. (All subsequent references to this edition, abbreviated *PM*.)

49

but it deliberately includes four writers to whom Lessing feels close: Brontë, Dostoievsky, Schreiner and Lawrence.) In some way their lives become an expression of revolt against those limitations they feel a bigoted, inhibited or absurd society attempts to impose upon them; they aspire to become 'free spirits'.[1] Where this revolt touches readers' lives they will feel a strong sense of identification with the literary figure, and there is no doubt that Lessing issues a clear invitation to do so in the first chapter of the opening novel, also with reference to Martha's own book-influenced sense of her self:

> . . . from these books Martha had gained a clear picture of herself, from the outside. She was adolescent, and therefore bound to be unhappy; British, and therefore uneasy and defensive; in the fourth decade of the twentieth century, and therefore inescapably beset with problems of race and class; female, and obliged to repudiate the shackled women of the past. She was tormented with guilt and responsibility and self-consciousness . . .[2]

This is a plain indication of the over-arching purpose of the sequence of five books, but it will come as no surprise to some readers that early critics of the first two parts were prone to abstract from this and stress the race problem or the theme of 'women's liberation' to neither of which has Lessing ever been exclusively committed. In an essay printed shortly after the first two books had appeared, she regretted the narrow responses they had met in England:

> Not one critic has understood what I should have thought would be obvious from the first chapter, where I was at pains to state the theme very clearly: that this is a study of the individual conscience in its relations with the collective. . . . As long as critics are 'sensitive', subjective, and uncommitted to anything but their own private sensibilities, there will be no body of criticism worth taking seriously in this country.[3]

But the distorted responses she complains of were partly due to her

[1] Martha's sense of herself as a 'free spirit' (*PM*, p. 145) reflects her awareness of her literary ancestry.

[2] *Martha Quest* (Panther edition, London, 1966), pp. 14, 15. (All subsequent references to this edition, abbreviated *MQ*.)

[3] 'The Small Personal Voice', in *Declaration*, ed. T. Maschler (MacGibbon & Kee, London, 1957), p. 22.

originality and vitality in treating the themes of race, sex, and marriage, partly to the very timeliness of her work. Now that the sequence is completed, it is possible to view it in the larger perspective she intended. However, since the theme of this study is Doris Lessing's Africa, not an exhaustive discussion of her work, I realize that there is a risk of similar distortion here. I hope to avoid this by prefacing discussion of the African aspect with a general survey of the sequence from stylistic and thematic viewpoints.

The form Lessing chose for 'Children of Violence' is not peculiar to her work, but is part of a modern tendency that has attracted many writers since Proust. Proust's series novel, under the collective title *À la Recherche du Temps Perdu*, extended to nine volumes, most of which were posthumously published in the nineteen twenties. He found in it an elastic and expansive form which enabled him to build round a central life, in this case a narrator-hero resembling the author, both intense individual experience and a complex web of society, interwoven with comment upon a seemingly infinite range of topics. The English novelist Anthony Powell, as the title of his series suggests, was influenced by Proust in conceiving his 'Music of Time' sequence, begun in 1951 and completed in 1976. Others who may be mentioned here are C. P. Snow, whose 'Strangers and Brothers' sequence is closer to Lessing's in its range of subject-matter, Joyce Cary, the author of two trilogies, Evelyn Waugh's trilogy of novels about the Second World War, 'Sword of Honour', Lawrence Durrell's 'Alexandria Quartet' (1957–60); the form is still alive in Edward Upward's political trilogy and a sequence by Frederic Raphael.

Lessing's handling of the form is less experimental than some of these, such as Powell, Durrell, and (in a less complicated way) Snow, who vary their viewpoint from novel to novel, experiment with time and deliberately undermine facile assumptions on the reader's part as to the nature of 'reality'. Such experimentation would have done little to further her purpose, as quoted above from 'The Small Personal Voice', which demanded a more orthodox realism and a more regular mode of narrative. The series novel (I am treating the five volumes as *one* novel for the purposes of this discussion) allowed her the amplitude and the elasticity she needed to trace in full detail the development of a life and of the 'atmosphere' of the times in which that life is lived.

This more clearly defined purpose sends us for a stronger affinity

51

in subject-matter rather than form, not to Proust, but to the German novel and, amongst the moderns, Thomas Mann. In an Author's Note at the end of the closing volume, *The Four-Gated City*, Lessing points out a connection that she evidently felt had been overlooked, though the sequence took eighteen years:

> This book is what the Germans call a *Bildungsroman*. This kind of novel has been out of fashion for some time: which does not mean that there is anything wrong with this kind of novel.[1]

Bildungsroman or 'educational novel'; the prototype is Goethe's *Wilhelm Meister*, in which – as in Lessing's work – the hero's school is society, his 'graduation' becoming fitted through the hard tests his individuality undergoes there to teach in his turn a fruitful relation between self and society. A closer modern affinity, however, is with Thomas Mann's *Der Zauberberg* (1924; trans. *The Magic Mountain*, 1927); I shall say more of the link with Mann in my later discussion of *The Four-Gated City*.

To return to the form: while some of the novelists I have mentioned seem to have worked through a potentially unlimited number of novels, Lessing's five-volume series has a clear, rounded structure, as does the traditional five-act play. Since the novel embraces a vision of society and of modern history, it can both cover a real span of time – from the mid-'thirties to the mid-'sixties – and take flight into the vision of the future, built on the known reality portrayed, with which the closing volume ends, involving also the end of Martha's life. There is space enough within this scheme to vary the amount of attention paid either to the heroine or her *milieu*.

The novel is entitled 'Children of Violence'. Its significance is suggested in the first book, *Martha Quest*, in the bewildered relationship between Martha and her parents who seem, her father especially, absorbed and psychologically disabled by the Great War. Their 'poetry of suffering'[2] casts a spell upon her, the would-be child of peace, that she will never shake off, though she may learn to live with it. Ten years and two broken marriages later, politically educated, carrying the painful knowledge that she can love men who choose violence, she comes to measure herself as a child of her time. She is conducting an imaginary argument with her one true

---

[1] *The Four-Gated City* (MacGibbon & Kee, London, 1969), p. 711. (All subsequent references to this edition, abbreviated *FGC*.)
[2] *MQ*, p. 32.

lover, the Polish Jew and refugee Thomas Stern, who has gone to Israel to fight the British:

> 'So, Martha,' she heard him say, conversational rather than aggressive, as if he were conducting a discussion in the current affairs group: 'So, you don't believe in violence, is that it?'
>
> Suppose one has loved a man or (however one wants to put it) been influenced by him, or (if you like) touched by him, but certainly in one's deepest self, and this man then picks up a gun and murders another man out of revenge, what does it mean, saying: I don't believe in violence?
>
> Having lived through a war when half the human race was engaged in murdering the other half, murdering more vilely, savagely, cruelly, than ever in human history, what does it mean to say: I don't believe that violence achieves anything?
>
> Every fibre of Martha's body, everything she thought, every movement she made, everything she was, was because she had been born at the end of one world war, and had spent all her adolescence in the atmosphere of preparations for another which had lasted five years and had inflicted such wounds on the human race that no one had any idea of what the results would be.
>
> Martha did not believe in violence.
>
> Martha was the essence of violence, she had been conceived, bred, fed and reared on violence.
>
> Martha argued with Thomas: What use is it, Thomas, what use is violence?[1]

At other times she walks out to her parents' house where her father lies in his final illness and her mother nurses him as she had in the War that brought them together:

> Sometimes Martha stood outside the fence and looked at the dark window and thought: that couple in there, that man and that woman, when they conceived me, one was in shellshock from the war, and the other in a breakdown from nursing its wounded. She, Martha, was as much a child of the 1914–1918 war as she was of Alfred Quest, May Quest.[2]

Martha's role of compassionate observer is her nearest possible

[1] *Landlocked* (Panther edition, 1965), p. 202. (All subsequent references to this edition, abbreviated *L*.)
[2] Ibid., p. 203.

approach to her parents in the flesh, by whose 'reactionary' racial, political and sexual attitudes she felt estranged even to the verge of destruction. She is bound to find a place to stand unsupported by them, to become *self* born; at first it is an inchoate urge – 'it was as if something new was demanding conception, with her flesh as host; as if it were a necessity, which she must bring herself to accept, that she should allow herself to dissolve and be formed by that necessity'[1] – but time and experience teach her how little choice she really has. The observation Mr. Maynard, the sardonic realist, makes at the end of *A Proper Marriage*, upon the break-up of her first marriage, is uncomfortably acute:

> I suppose with the French Revolution for a father and the Russian Revolution for a mother, you can very well dispense with a family. . . .[2]

With such 'parents' it is no wonder that Martha searches continually for love, to bring about her rebirth: the closing volume, *The Four-Gated City*, is an attempt to point the way, a way beyond the scope of one life that 'new children' may know.

Martha's searching role is obviously pointed by the name of Quest, an unashamedly old-fashioned, allegorical way of indicating Lessing's purpose. One might compare one of the best known allegories in English, *Pilgrim's Progress*, similarly based on the familiar metaphor of life as a journey. In that case, as in this, the author's knowledge of human nature and capacity for realistic narrative was not inhibited by the convention. Unlike Bunyan, the naming stops with the heroine: the other characters in the series are not named in a similar way, which would for today's readership have certainly undermined the sense of reality. The five books correspond to five definable stages in Martha's journey through life: *Martha Quest* opens with questioning adolescence and ends with her first independent moves, into work and marriage, from the soil to the city; *A Proper Marriage* shows her first venture into freedom and her first trial of love to be illusory and ends with her renewed search for a fuller life in a 'collective' purpose; in *A Ripple from the Storm* she makes full trial of this ideal in the divided world of political reality and contracts a second marriage in the same divided spirit; *Landlocked* marks her failure, though she deepens her experience of love, to come into possession of either a fulfilling

---

[1] *MQ*, p. 62.
[2] *PM*, p. 380.

personal or 'collective' world, but despite these frustrations she still has the will to seek beyond her African world; *The Four-Gated City* is set in London, where even to the catastrophic end Martha explores ways, through her relations with others or in her deepest self, to live differently; the 'Appendix' to this final book, partly set in Africa, is projected into a catastrophic future, but the metaphysical pattern of the novel comes full circle with the culmination of a vision that runs from the first chapter of the series throughout, the vision of the four-gated city.[1] To carry out her wider intentions, one can see why Lessing translated Martha to London in the last book: it is a centre of world history, not, like Zambesia, a minor offshoot. Understanding London, England – a centre of that great, flawed civilization which could mother the malformed society of Zambesia – involves examining the diseased heart, tracing the sickness to its source. It is seen with a disenchanted eye formed in Africa, as dispassionately observant as those eyes Lessing's children turn upon their flawed elders in the *African Stories*.

The portrayal of a life like Martha's, which responds intensely to all facets of experience, enables Lessing to deal naturally with a great variety of modern situations and problems, both major and minor. These are pursued over a span of thirty years and convey a multifarious sense of the moving age. If the original perspective, that of a parochial settlerdom, is narrow, it furthers the purpose: the reader's perspectives enlarge with Martha's, her expanding relationships gradually involving major issues and events of our time. An impromptu list would include colonialism, black and white relationships, changing sexual attitudes – closely bound up throughout with the 'remarkable traffic between parents and children'[2] – anti-Semitism and Zionism, the several faces of Communism, the drift since the Second World War in the shadow of The Bomb, the protest movement against it (in Britain), the psychology of despair, changing views of what constitutes 'sanity' or 'normal' behaviour, and attempts to confront the dark future. Keeping pace with the unfolding action is a running series of allusive quotations placed as epigraphs at the beginning of each part of each book. These serve various purposes: to point suggestive parallels between the present and the past, to place Martha's experience in the wider human context, to provide further

---

[1] Introduced in *MQ*, p. 17. (I shall enlarge upon this in Chapter 6.)
[2] *FGC*, p. 493.

perspectives from literary, psychological or political texts especially relevant to the themes as they develop. This technique is akin to the common Victorian practice, but it is used more sparingly by Lessing (as by other modern writers who have revived it, perhaps following T. S. Eliot's example in *The Waste Land*): George Eliot must have been hard pressed to find fifty suitable epigraphs, one for each *chapter* of *Felix Holt* (1866). Also, unlike the Victorian novelist, Lessing uses the technique strictly as a means of bringing out the thematic significance of the action.

Before closing this general survey of the novel's form and themes, I should like to dispose briefly of an aspect which may occur to the reader – recalling my sketch of the author's life in Chapter 1 – but which I prefer to set aside. This is the temptation to a 'biographical reading' of the series suggested by the obvious similarities between the author's life and her heroine's: their shared date of birth (October 1919); parents of whom one was a First World War army officer obsessed with his war experience, the other a nurse he met during that War and married after; Martha's two marriages and divorces, involving a Civil Servant and a European refugee; departure for England at the age of 30 – after which the last book yields no such obvious parallels. What does this mean? Nothing more *for art*, than that an author draws in part upon her life for her subject matter, but Lessing had reason to object when 'Children of Violence' was being published that reviewers used such resemblances between author and heroine to reduce discussion of the novel to a 'gossip-column level where the heroine ... was equated with me, compared with me, and my views assumed to be hers.'[1] Obviously, it is a short step from reading fiction as disguised autobiography to converting it into autobiography pure and simple – to no valuable end, since it eludes ultimate proof. Such excursions may be inevitable because authors' lives interest us, but cannot pass for useful criticism of the work of art. Lessing may well have hoped to avoid such futile responses by abstaining – unlike such other writers of series novels as Proust, Powell and Durrell – from either casting her protagonist as a novelist or employing a novelist as narrator within the series.[2]

---

[1] 'Footnote to *The Golden Notebook*', interview by Robert Rubens, *The Queen's*, 21 August 1962, p. 31. Lessing allows herself a lengthy digression against biographical reading in *FGC*, pp. 520–1.

[2] Mark Coldridge, the novelist in *FGC*, functions in neither of these roles. In *The Golden Notebook* she does portray the heroine as novelist, but still gives no excuse for crude biographical readings.

6   Children of Violence:
Dream and Reality

In the previous chapter I quoted Lessing's statement from 'The Small Personal Voice' that the clear theme of *Children of Violence* was 'a study of the individual conscience in its relation with the collective'. As a generalization, this could be applied to the whole class of novels such as hers, which explore the individual's growth to selfhood in conflict with the larger society, a kind of novel especially characteristic of our time. Within this broad category, however, there are infinite possibilities of variation. What *is* 'the individual conscience': where does it spring from, is it free or conditioned by circumstance and heredity? 'Circumstance' includes 'the collective', broadly the society in which the individual develops, which we may regard as the antagonist: how far does the particular nature of the 'collective' determine individual action? Many novelists have found themselves obliged to confront these teasing questions: to explore the very nature of individuality, of 'freedom', which they realize is not to be taken for granted. A much quoted generalization, made by George Eliot in her political novel *Felix Holt* (1866), aptly confronts us with the issue: 'There is no private life which has not been determined by a wider public life.'[1] In Lessing, as in Eliot, the element of determinism, embodying restraints upon individualism by what Lessing (using a phrase derived from Marxist terminology) terms the collective, is so strong that the possibility of the individual freedom remains an open question to the end. The whole issue is complicated by the fact that few but the most extreme individuals desire utter separation from the collective.

Treating it thus, as I have suggested, Lessing is at one with many modern novelists: Conrad, Gide, Faulkner, Mann, Huxley, Woolf, Joyce Cary, Kafka, Golding, V. S. Naipaul, to name only a few who write with an obvious consciousness of the problem. Apart from

---

[1] *Felix Holt*, Chapter III.

their techniques, these writers each naturally explore it from viewpoints formed by their individual experiences of time and place and directed by that mysterious entity, 'the individual conscience'. The most obviously distinctive quality of Lessing's work so far as subject-matter is concerned is that it derives from an Africa in which she grew up (unlike Cary, who wrote of Nigeria out of mature experience only, as a District Officer) in a state of isolation from broad cultural influences rare for a white society in our time. It is an experience that can never be repeated, now that the last enclaves of white settlerdom outside South Africa are in their death throes. So little had changed between her childhood and that of Olive Schreiner, growing up on the South African veld in the late nineteenth century, that *Martha Quest* seems to take up the thread where Schreiner dropped it in *The Story of an African Farm* (1883). Martha inherits the very same problems that bedevilled Schreiner's Lyndall: both struggled to find food for their spirits, striving outward from a narrow, constricting world at first in literature, then in painful experiments in love; in both the woman feels the restriction most; and in both novelists there developed a passionate involvement in the South African racial issue – in Schreiner, of course, after *The Story of an African Farm* was published. At bottom, both share the African soil and their 'individual conscience' is profoundly nourished by it.

Behind the writings of Schreiner and Lessing, and in White African literature in general, one can detect what may be called The African Dream. This is as many-sided as its much more debated counterpart, the American Dream. In both cases the Dream was fed by a disillusionment with what is and the eternal hope for what might be, in another country, 'unspoilt', untainted by a corrupt civilization. Hence, the powerful myth of the Noble African, the good child of Nature, unfallen man, which held sway for several centuries while contact with Africa was more legendary than real. As exploration and conquest in Africa increased the white man's knowledge – and as his own growing power increased his sense of superiority – the nobler myths gradually gave way to those that stamped the African as a *child* of nature, who need paternal guidance, and as a retarded branch of the human race which needed civilizing. In the nineteenth century, these myths became political necessities, whether sincerely held or not, particularly in those parts of Africa which held out promise of material wealth and even living space for the overcrowded populations of Europe. Among the most attractive parts of Africa for white settlement and exploitation were the South and the East, in what are now the countries of South Africa, Uganda, Kenya, Zambia (Northern Rhodesia), Tanzania (Tanganyika), Malawi and Lessing's Southern Rhodesia (the future African State of Zimbabwe). In all these countries there was considerable white settlement from the late nineteenth century on.

It would be a mistake to assert that all white settlers were drawn to Africa by cynically materialistic motives, though many of those who joined the gold rush must have had no other. We have seen that Lessing portrays relatively few of these, but her subject is rather those who were drawn by the land, the prospect of unlimited space, the possibilities of solitude and independence, the challenge of breaking new ground. Her whites are often romantics, dreaming as does Alec Barnes in 'Eldorado' (and her own father) of 'distance'. They and their forerunners had felt the beckoning of the challenging invitation issued by that most complex of African adventurers, Cecil Rhodes, to go north from the settled provinces of South Africa and open up what later became the Rhodesias:

> He told the settlers, and he so clearly meant it, that he believed with all his mind and heart in the North that was theirs. Surely, he said to them later, but he said much the same to them now and always, surely to be here was 'a happier thing than the deadly monotony of an English country town or the still dealier monotony of a Karroo village. Here, at any rate, you have your share in the creation of a new country. . . . You have the proud satisfaction of knowing that you are civilizing a new part of the world. Those who fall in that creation fall sooner than they would in ordinary lives, but their lives are better and grander.'
> And to a friend he (later too) said: 'How glorious this is, and how lucky you are to be here! But why are you here? Because turnips did not pay in ——shire. Had they paid, you would have remained an average country gentleman and a fairly respectable Member of Parliament. How much better to be here under the stars, thinking out great problems!' . . .[1]

This was the most potent of dreams: new wealth *and* 'civilization', that paradoxical combination of freebooting colonization and the missionary spirit which seems to later generations merely hypocritical. Of course, they did not know their limitations; they did not foresee that their 'superiority' was only a temporary

[1] Sarah Gertrude Millin, *Rhodes* (London, 1933), pp. 164–5.

advantage, that they were not a race of supermen. They would become an apprehensive, closed minority, defending their position with clichés about 'them' – the untrustworthy, 'ungrateful', 'lazy' native in those ceaseless catechisms Martha overhears her mother exchanging with her neighbours during her childhood. By the nineteen twenties the bold dream of vast new settlements had turned into rural humdrum or the new English suburbia of cities like Salisbury and Bulawayo, the home from home so sharply satirized in 'A Home for the Highland Cattle' and *A Proper Marriage*. What began as an urge for new freedom has ended in caged, fearful confinement.

Martha, the child – with a chance, like all children, to 'live differently' – sees this and rebels in the only direction open to her, into solitude, closeness to the natural world, ironically like many a romantic settler before her. It is here that we find the deepest source of 'her' Africa, but it is one to which we can point, it will not be probed. Martha herself attempts to measure it against that literary experience which she so often uses as a test of reality:

> In the literature that was her tradition, the word *farm* evokes an image of something orderly, compact, cultivated; a neat farmhouse in a pattern of fields. Martha looked over a mile or so of bush to a strip of pink ploughed land; and then the bush, dark green and sombre, climbed a ridge to another patch of exposed earth, this time a clayish yellow; and then, ridge after ridge, fold after fold, the bush stretched to a line of blue kopjes. The fields were a timid intrusion on a landscape hardly marked by man; and the hawk which circled in mile-wide sweeps over her head saw the house, crouched on its long hill, the cluster of grass huts which was the native compound huddled on a lower rise half a mile away; perhaps a dozen patches of naked soil – and then nothing to disturb that ancient, down-peering eye, nothing that a thousand generations of his hawk ancestors had not seen.[1]

The contrasting 'tradition' is, of course, the English; compare George Eliot's comment on the 'one with nature' childhood experience common to herself and her heroine, Maggie Tulliver:

> The wood I walk in on this mild May day, with the young yellow-brown foliage of the oaks between me and the blue sky, the white star-flowers and the blue-eyed speedwell and the

[1] *MQ*, p. 8.

ground ivy at my feet – what grove of tropic palms, what strange ferns or splendid broad-petalled blossoms, could ever thrill such deep and delicate fibres within me as this home scene? These familiar flowers, these well-remembered bird-notes, this sky, with its fitful brightness, these furrowed and grassy fields, each with a sort of personality given to it by the capricious hedgerows – such things as these are the mother tongue of our imagination, the language that is laden with all the subtle inextricable associations the fleeting hours of our childhood left behind them. Our delight in the sunshine on the deep-bladed grass to-day might be no more than the faint perception of wearied souls, if it were not for the sunshine and the grass in the far-off years which still live in us, and transform our perception into love.[1]

The contrast is one between nature ordered, tamed, lovable and a nature untameably vast, beyond man's shaping. Maggie Tulliver's 'perception', we are told, will ripen into love; the sentiment is Wordsworthian, reminiscent of Wordsworth's passionate 'a feeling and a love' that garner 'food for future years'. Martha is overwhelmed by a feeling less definable and by no means soothing; of her birth month, weighted with heat, she feels: 'How terrible October is! Terrible because so beautiful, and the beauty springs from the loaded heat, the dust, the tension . . . She sat there all day, and felt the waves of heat and perfume break across her in shock after shock of shuddering nostalgia. But nostalgia for what?'[2] Nature drugs and repels; she tries vainly to reduce it to human scale:

> She read the same books over and over again, in between intervals of distracted daydreaming, in a trance of recognition, and in always the same place, under the big tree that was her refuge, through which the heat pumped like a narcotic. She read poetry, not for the sense of the words, but for the melodies which confirmed the rhythm of the moving grasses and the swaying of the leaves over her head, or the ideal landscape of white cities and noble people which lay over the actual vistas of harsh grass and stunted trees like a golden mirage.[3]

This is the imaginative aspect of her dream, her urge to reshape

[1] *The Mill on the Floss* (1860), Chapter V.
[2] *MQ*, pp. 28–9.
[3] *MQ*, p. 35.

existence. There is another, less conscious, for which there are no adequate words. The key passage is too lengthy to quote here; it may be called, variously and only approximately, a moment of 'ecstasy' or 'illumination' – or, more rationally, 'difficult knowledge':

> There was a slow integration, during which she, and the little animals, and the moving grasses, and the sunwarmed trees, and the slopes of shivering silvery mealies, and the great dome of blue light overhead, and the stones of earth under her feet, become one, shuddering together in a dissolution of dancing atoms. She felt the rivers under the ground forcing themselves painfully along her veins, swelling them out in an unbearable pressure; her flesh was the earth, and suffered growth like a ferment; and her eyes stared, fixed like the eye of the sun. . . .
>
> . . . There had been a challenge that she had refused. But the wave of nostalgia made her angry. She knew it to be a falsity; for it was a longing for something that had never existed, an 'ecstasy', in short. There had been no ecstasy, only difficult knowledge. It was as if a beetle had sung. There should be a new word for *illumination*.[1]

Afterwards, Martha feels irritation with the consciousness that her 'moment' defies description but *invites* falsification; she tries to resist naming it with such Wordsworthian words as 'joy' or 'sublimity'. Nevertheless, it remains as the measure of much that she *can* define as she matures and lives increasingly cut off from the soil:

> . . . as she read she asked herself, What has this got to do with me? Mostly, she rejected; what she accepted she took instinctively, for it rang true with some tuning fork to guide within her; and the measure was that experience (she thought of it as one, though it was the fusion of many, varying in intensity) which was the gift of her solitary childhood on the veld: that knowledge of something painful and ecstatic, something central and fixed, but flowing. It was a sense of movement, of separate things interacting and finally becoming one, but greater – it was this which was her lodestone, even her conscience; and so, when she put down this book, that author, it was with the simplicity of perfect certainty, like the

[1] *MQ*, p. 62. The key passage covers pp. 61–3 (Chapter Two).

certainties of ignorance: It isn't true. And so these authors, these philosophers who had fed and maintained (or so she understood) so many earlier generations, were discarded with the ease with which she had shed religion: they wouldn't do, or not for her.[1]

Her solitary life on the veld, those intense intimations of oneness – the self in accord with its world and 'understanding' it at its heart – is linked with Martha's 'conscience'. Once again, but in terms rather of affinity than difference, one is reminded of Wordsworth's record in his autobiographical poem in *The Prelude* of those 'spots of time' that most profoundly though inexplicably impressed him and were to remain as moral bearings in later life. A few lines from 'Tintern Abbey' will point the connection in spirit if not in language, where he speaks of being –

> . . . Well pleased to recognise
> In nature and the language of the sense
> The anchor of my purest thoughts, the nurse,
> The guide, the guardian of my heart, and soul
> Of all my moral being.[2]

I have laboured the Wordsworthian links somewhat because it seems important to give Lessing her true bearings within the English Romantic tradition of which he is an acknowledged father and of which her bookish heroine is aware; further, as one who also writes of the conflict between the dictates of his individual conscience, which he repeatedly links with what for the want of a better word must be called his 'ecstatic' experience of Nature, and the social conscience, as influenced by people, ideas, literature.[3] It is not an easy opposition to define, and I have only roughly sketched it, but it indicates the essential bearings of a complex tradition relative to which we may understand the relationship between dream and reality in Lessing's work. The transcendental idealists, Whitman and Thoreau, Martha reads at this time are a nearer part of the tradition, as is the Schreiner of *The Story of an African Farm*. Part Two of Schreiner's novel opens with a record of the 'seasons' of 'the soul's life' and traces its growth into a sense of Nature's oneness.

I have referred to Martha's consciousness of the risks of labelling

[1] *MQ*, p. 220.
[2] 'Lines' (1798), ll. 107–111.
[3] Book V of *The Prelude* is entitled 'Books'.

the moment: her modern form of self-consciousness keeps her aware of the dangerous attraction of what, commenting on Wordsworth, Keats dubbed 'the egotistical sublime'; nor can she say 'soul'. Lessing clearly stands behind her here; she notes in a book review from the 'fifties: 'An African once said to me that beyond all the white man's more obvious crimes in Africa there was the unforgivable one that "even the best of you use Africa as a peg to hang your egos on". To this charge Mr. Van der Post is open. So are all the rest of us.'[1] Martha's 'ecstasy' would illustrate the charge, but her guarded response to it is her defence. The worst danger, of which Lessing finds Van Der Post guilty, is to fall into the pathetic fallacy, endowing Nature with human emotions; this is the weaker side of Wordsworth (though he himself knew better) and of Wordsworthian*ism*. Reviewing another of Van der Post's popular books of African travel and exploration, she ridicules his pathetic fallacies and 'one-sided' irrationalism and utters the heartfelt – 'The African landscape is still, thank God, impersonal and indifferent to man.'[2] This statement illustrates her strong affinity with Thomas Hardy, that great sceptical inheritor of the Wordsworthian tradition, who corrected its extravagances sharply in his caustic authorial comments on 'Nature's holy plan' in *Tess of the d'Urbervilles* (1891): if Nature *has* a plan, it is no more than 'the survival of the fittest', who may or may not be the best. Man may work with Nature, mould it to his needs, but it will not be by Nature's gift that he succeeds; the human is the determining factor. This has already been pointed out in my comments on her earlier work; it is brought out in *Martha Quest* in the extended portrayal of Mr. Quest's failure to come to terms with the earth. Perhaps the intense feeling for the landscape that Martha experiences is conditional upon childhood and solitude; though later social forms and settlement will close in upon her, she will never lose that complete, passionate confrontation with Nature: that at least she can claim as her sole individual possession. In changing forms, she will struggle to cling to it.

Only when it is behind her, when she has become increasingly absorbed into the 'collective' urban life, does she come to measure its value; the closing chapters of the first book include a valedictory vision of what she will lose as she is about to embark on her first

---

[1]'Desert Child', *New Statesman*, 56, 15 November 1958, p. 700: review of Laurens Van Der Post, *The Lost World of the Kalahari*.
[2]'African Interiors', *New Statesman*, 62, 27 October 1961, pp. 613–14: review of L. Van Der Post, *The Heart of the Hunter*.

marriage with the 'sensible young man whom it was so easy to love'; they are driving out to the Quest farm so that Douglas may meet her parents:

> The sky was deep and blue and fresh as a sweep of sea, and the white clouds rolled steadily in it. The veld, so thickly clothed with grass, broken with small tumbling kopjes which glittered with hot granite boulders, lifted itself unafraid to meet that sky. This naked embrace of earth and sky, the sun hard and strong overhead, pulling up the moisture from foliage, from soil, so that the swimming glisten of heat is like a caress made visible, this openness of air, everything visible for leagues, so that the circling hawk (the sun glancing off its wings) seems equipoised between sun and boulder – this frank embrace between the lifting breast of the land and the deep blue warmth of the sky is what exiles from Africa dream of; it is what they sicken for, no matter how hard they try to shut their minds against the memory of it. And what if one sickens for it when one still lives in Africa, one chooses to remain in town? Living in town, Martha had forgotten this infinite exchange of earth and sky.[1]

This spacious vision is an utter contrast to the human entanglements she stands on the verge of: where can one find its counterpart in the human world? For that spaciousness she exchanges, as Mrs. Knowell, the box-like flat in the heart of the drab colonial town and attempts to call ancestral styles of living to her aid. 'For instance, there was her father's childhood in the English country cottage, honest simplicity with the bones of the house showing through lathe and plaster. Outside, a green and lush country – but tame, tamed; it would not do at all.'[2] When her father moves, a sick man, to the town, her last claim to the veld is broken:

> . . . Martha felt an exile, as he did. She did not know how much it had meant that her parents, at least, had been on the land. Some balance had been upset in her. That fatal dichotomy, soil, city, had been at least held even by thinking of her father working his land. Now she felt altogether cut off from her roots, even more so because she disliked the idea of actually living on a farm so much.[3]

[1] *MQ*, p. 252.
[2] *PM*, p. 76.
[3] *PM*, p. 146.

The last sentence carries again the ironic note of reservation: the farm itself was confining, but it had been at least the gateway to free space. She asks herself, as her marriage and social life grow stale and repetitive, and she finds herself turning willy nilly to her pathetic patch of urban garden, usurping the garden boy's task:

> And why was it that nothing but the veld she had been brought up on, the sere, empty, dry vleis, the scrubby little trees, the enormous burnt windy spaces of the high veld, could satisfy her feeling for what nature should be? Dryness, barrenness, stunted growth, the colours that are fed from starved roots – thin browns and greys, dull greens and sad yellows – and all under a high, dry, empty sky: these were what she craved. The thoughts of a planned and comfortable country, filled with prosperous villas in green and fruitful acres, was dismaying and distasteful.[1]

It is a question Martha cannot herself answer: only her life can answer it.

This passage is the last in the series of novels in which Martha's African landscape dominates her imagination; it comes toward the end of the second book. Up to that point and beyond it has been increasingly encroached upon by the outer life, so that it is driven inward and becomes a despairing metaphor for her lost freedom. As the series progresses, we see it gradually replaced by other metaphors which yet have an essential kinship with it, whose significance helps to define what 'the veld' really meant. In the third book, *The Ripple from the Storm*, the most political of the novels, she finds a temporary panacea in her dream of the Soviet Union, another country rendered attractive by space, distance, ignorance of its reality – 'over there it's all finished, race prejudice and anti-Semitism'.[2] Though it takes her years to realize it, that dream will turn to nightmare. Meanwhile, her unconscious mind provides an, as yet, indecipherable alternative; like all Lessing's heroines, her dream life attempts to supply meaning where her conscious life is failing her.

> She had been dreaming and she wished she might return to sleep, for the dreams had had the peculiarly nostalgic quality which she distrusted so much, and yet was so dangerously attractive to her. She had been dreaming of 'that country', . . .

[1] *PM*, p. 282.
[2] *RFS*, p. 27.

'that country' was pale, misted, flat; gulls cried like children around violet-coloured shores. She stood on coloured chalky rocks with a bitter sea washing around her feet and the smell of salt was strong in her nostrils.

Now she thought: Well, I suppose it's England . . . but how can I be an exile from England when it has nothing to do with me?[1]

The sea replaces the veld in her imagination; it strengthens in *Landlocked*, the fourth book, as her search for freedom in political change and in love runs dry and she turns away from Africa, even the veld.

The sea was her sleep now, she went off to sleep returning to her old nurse, the sea. She was becoming obsessed with the sea, which she had not seen, did not remember. She had only to shut her eyes and waves lifted and crashed across her eyelids and an enormous, longing joy took possession of her. She no longer thought: I'm going to England soon; she thought: I'm going to the sea, I'm going to get off this high, dry place where my skin burns and where I can never lose the feeling of tension and I shall sit by a long, grey sea and listen to the waves break, I shall hear the waves break and sink in a small hiss of foam.[2]

But there will be no such clean break; the sea is a metaphor for that inner need which the veld once satisfied. As the veld gave way to the limiting town, so the sea will bring her to England, London, and a renewal of the 'collective' limits. With regard to the sea-veld relationship, it seems worthwhile to interject the witness of another white writer whose experience of Africa, in Kenya, parallels Lessing's – but in reverse; this is the Danish writer, Karen Blixen (Isak Dinesen) who writes at the end of her excellent introduction to an edition of Schreiner's *The Story of an African Farm*:

I was once, when I was home from Africa on a visit, asked to give in two words an explanation of that charm of Africa which would draw me back to her in spite of many privations and failures. I could find none better than these: Nobility, Wideness. There is a great perspective in the landscape, as in existence, in Africa. The wideness of her plains has in it such

[1]*RFS*, p. 95.
[2]*L*, p. 206.

freedom and such promise, that I myself, who have been born and bred by the sea, and in Europe find it difficult to live away from it, in Africa never missed it.[1]

Freedom, imagination, promise, scope for dreams: the veld and the sea are two forms of the *terra incognita* that allow space for the individual's making. Yet these are not the only forms of possibility; man is torn between 'two desires':

> One drives him to the world without,
> And one to solitude.[2]

All romantic spirits feel this conflict. In Martha it is never finally resolved; the dialectic between the individual conscience and the collective continues to the end. Though in the final book, *The Four-Gated City*, she renews in England her commitments to her fellow beings and holds fast to it until her death, that book also traces in her middle age the most inward exploration she has made. Her 'new territory' is not 'Martha's mind', but the infinitely wide 'human mind'[3] and in her risky exploration of it she discovers a new 'Africa' which she comes to see as the true 'collective', though it will take many generations beyond her own for humanity to come into possession of it. So far it is almost entirely a dark continent. To see this in fuller perspective, I shall retrace my steps somewhat and pay more attention to the idea of 'the four-gated city', the idea or ideal which symbolizes the 'collective' aspect of Martha's vision and the crucial meeting-point (as it is in our civilization) of the dream and the reality.

Here we have no continuing city, but we seek one to come[4]

I have so far concentrated on the desire of the solitary individual to achieve a sense of unity which cannot be felt in the disordered life of human society, yet this very desire implies another desire, for a whole, harmonious society to which that individual could happily belong. The two desires are the two sides of the same idealist's coin, or the two poles between which the idealist oscillates. In this respect, as in her passionate communion with nature, Martha Quest

---

[1]Limited Editions Society edition of *The Story of an African Farm* (Westerham Press, England, 1961), p. xii.
[2]Matthew Arnold, 'Stanzas in Memory of the Author of *Obermann*' (1852).
[3]*FGC*, p. 546.
[4]S. Paul, *Epistle to the Hebrews*, xiii. 14.

is living a universal experience, but within an environmental context and with modern variations that make hers unique. Lessing comments in 'A Home for the Highland Cattle' how, at the annual ceremony to mark the founding of the town the pioneers established beneath the kopje, there springs 'in the minds of the listeners . . . a vision of that city *we all* [my italics] dream of, that planned and shapely city without stain or slum . . .'.[1] The sordid reality, sixty years later, is a sad, ironic contrast with that dream of a perfect city Rhodes had cherished. Freedom and order: Africa's unlimited potential was to have given Western man new scope for this; the freedom of space, the order of the ideal, planned city placed in it, an utter contrast to the chaotic, crowded cities of the old country.

Thus, one part of Lessing's purpose is her ironic depiction of the fate of that side of the dream. The other, more positive, springs from her enduring belief, as strong in her as history shows it has been in mankind as a whole, that the ideal city must be kept alive in the imagination. It is, of course, the utopian vision, or, in religious terms, the vision of the Celestial City: both, for 'utopia' means 'nowhere', have always had to be envisioned as out of this world we know, or at best postponed to an indefinite future. No simple minded idealist, Lessing has nevertheless striven to bring her readers to contemplate this ancient vision afresh, to hold in view a 'vision of the good' and not to be drawn into 'the pleasurable luxury of despair, the acceptance of disgust' which has become typical of so much of the most admired Western literature of alienation in the Post-War period; she set herself instead 'to re-write the old utopias'.[2]

Just as in her early experience of the veld Martha, though she doesn't know it, is reliving the romantic African Dream, so in turning away from the problems that beset her as a human being and 'female' in 'the fourth decade of the twentieth century' to build on that veld a vision of an ideal community, she is following the imaginative path of a Rhodes and countless dreamers before him. The image is established in the first chapter of the sequence:

> [Martha] looked away over the ploughed land, across the veld to the Dumfries Hills, and refashioned that unused country to the scale of her imagination. There arose, glimmering whitely over the harsh scrub and the stunted

[1] *Five*, op. cit., p. 11.
[2] *Declaration*, op. cit., pp. 19–20. She singles out, as authors of despair, Sartre, Genet, Beckett, Camus.

trees, a noble city, set foursquare and colonnaded along its falling flower-bordered terraces. There were splashing fountains, and the sound of flutes; and its citizens moved, grave and beautiful, black and white and brown together; and these groups of elders paused, and smiled with pleasure at the sight of children – the blue-eyed, fair-skinned children of the North playing hand in hand with the bronze-skinned, dark-eyed children of the South. Yes, they smiled and approved these many-fathered children, running and playing among the flowers and the terraces, through the white pillars and tall trees of this fabulous and ancient city. . . .[1]

This is Martha's dream of that ideal life with which she would supplant the fretful, apprehensive existence of her people uneasily controlling 'them' – the 'natives'. As we shall see, the image of that city runs as a *leit motiv* through the series and gives the final book its title.

Martha's dream could not be entirely her own; her reading must have fed it and its main elements must be deeply embedded in the human mind. Among the ideal cities to which hers is related are the 'foursquare' holy city, 'the new Jerusalem' of St. John's vision,[2] Andreae's Christianopolis, Sir Thomas More's Amaurote, the four-gated Sun City of Campanella and – part of the African Dream – Timbuktu. Martha's modern utopia would solve the problems that beset her age: the children of her city should be, not only children of the community, but children of peace (she herself is consciously the child of violence) and miscegenation. The dark and light children hand in hand recall Blake's poem, 'The Little Black Boy'. Blake was a keen emancipist, a devotee of Swedenborg who wished to establish the Church of New Jerusalem in Africa. Utopists from Swedenborg to the late nineteenth-century rationalist Theodor Hertzka's Edenvale colony, have placed in Africa their Eden Regained (not a continuation of the Noble African myth, but rather a Western vision of Africa's potential, as the Unknown, for a new nobility). Like theirs, Martha's is essentially a reactionary utopia, neat, limited, self-sufficient. Lessing has admitted to such visions herself – compare the passage in *Going Home* where she recalls one of Capetown seen, from above and afar as a 'free and illuminated' city[3] – but she chastens them with a dry, ironic light.

[1] *MQ*, p. 17.
[2] *The Revelation of S. John the Divine*, xxi.
[3] *Going Home*, op. cit., pp. 56–7.

Martha, her utopian quester, is as intransigent in pursuing her vision as any adolescent utopist has ever been: 'Outside one of the gates stood her parents, the Van Rensbergs, in fact most of the people of the district, forever excluded from the golden city because of their pettiness of vision and small understanding.'[1] Caught up in the toils of reaction against what is, she at first takes too exalted a view of her mission, which Lessing treats in mock-heroic style. In her anxiously transfiguring eyes even the Van Rensbergs' clod-hopping Saturday dance, her first social event, is 'magnified . . . peopled with youthful beings who had less to do with what was likely than with that vision of legendary cities which occupied so much of her imagination'.[2] From there, her virginal, self-made dress torn and muddied, she resolves to turn her back on this stagnant life of the veld, where it seems that 'the time for the creations of legends is past'[3] and put her trust in the colonial metropolis as a source of '*new* life'.

In these early chapters a good-humoured authorial irony plays over Martha's naïveté, but it is more astringent when directed upon the unworthy objective of her quest; Martha will not become, with Paul, 'a citizen of no mean city'[4]:

> Founders' Street was narrow and shabby; and though it was named to commemorate those adventurers who came riding over the veld to plant the Union Jack, regardless of the consequences to themselves or anyone else, it was now synonymous in the minds of the present citizens with dubious boarding-houses and third-rate shops.[5]

Nevertheless, Martha can convert Rhodes's legacy into genuine gold: 'though the pavement was a dull city pavement, the posters on the walls . . . garish . . . the place was transformed into something very like one of her private dreams'.[6] For a while she lives it up with the gilded youth, finds living itself an end, but the something more soon reasserts itself – though also in forms weakly resembling the ideal; she attaches herself to a pink Socialist group whose sacred rag is *The New Statesman*, devouring which reawakens her dream of the

[1] *MQ*, p. 17.
[2] *MQ*, p. 73.
[3] *MQ*, p. 54.
[4] *The Acts of the Apostles*, xxi. 39.
[5] *MQ*, p. 93.
[6] *MQ*, p. 117.

'broad-thoroughfared, tree-lined, four-gated dignified city'.[1]

Actually, there is no connection: she snatches as she can at the slightest means of defining herself against the 'governing classes' of the city, the utmost reach of whose imagination is to plant a simulacrum of the Old Country's suburbia in the middle of the veld, with a Sports Club to give 'tone' and where the most lively conversations concern the 'native' problem. Desiring to belong to an ampler life, Martha throws herself into marrying Douglas Knowell, at bottom a conforming member of the establishment, out of no stronger an affinity than a shared subscription to *The New Statesman* and the Left Book Club: she is a child of the 'thirties. It was a time when many, such as those who went out to the Spanish Civil War (like Joss, the Jewish idealist in *Martha Quest*), gave themselves freely, naïvely, to whatever nearest cause seemed worthy. Like them, Martha always needs community, a quality that distinguishes her most sharply from the alienated protagonists so typical of the contemporary novels Lessing disapproves of: the testing and chastening of that need in *Children of Violence* becomes an object lesson for modern idealists.

The fruits of the colonial education she later carries with her to London become evident in a key passage of *The Four-Gated City* in which she is able to supply with the full authority of her own developed character the chastened corollary to Mark Coldridge's vision of the archetypal city:

> Great roads approached the city, from north and south, east and west. When they had fairly entered it, they divided into arcs, making a circling street, inside which were small ones: a web of arcs intersected by streets running in to a centre. All these streets were wide, paved with stone, lined by trees. The centre was planted with trees and had buildings in the trees. These were schools and libraries and market-places, but their functions were not over-defined. People might teach in the market; and in what looked like a temple, or a place of worship, goods could be bought or bartered for. Carpets for instance, or jewellery, or poems. There was no central building to the city, yet the people maintained that somewhere in it was such a lode-place or nodal point – under the city perhaps; perhaps in some small not apparently significant room in one of the libraries, or off a market. Or it could have been that the common talk about this room was

[1] *MQ*, p. 134.

another way of putting their belief that there existed people, in this city, who formed a kind of centre, almost a variety of powerhouse, who had no particular function or title, but who kept it in existence. The city had been planned as a whole once, long ago: had been built as a whole. It had not grown into existence, haphazard, as we are accustomed to think of cities doing. Every house in it had been planned, and who would live in each house. Every person in the city had a function and a place; but there was nothing static about this society: people could move out and up and into other functions, if they wished to. It was a gardened city. A great number of the inhabitants spent their lives on the gardens, and the fountains and parks. Even the trees and plants were known for their properties and qualities and grown exactly, in a relation to other plants, and to people and buildings; and it was among the gardeners, so the stories went, that could be found, if only one could recognize them, most of the hidden people who protected and fed the city.

'And all this,' said Mark, stating his position, 'went on for thousands of years – until, one day, there was an accident, something as senseless and stupid as an earthquake which swallowed the city, or a meteor from space.'

'Oh no,' said Martha, stating her position, 'around that city, just like all the cities we know, like Johannesburg for instance, grew up a shadow city of poverty and beastliness. A shanty town. Around that marvellous ordered city, another one of hungry and dirty and short-lived people. And one day the people of the outer city overran the inner one, and destroyed it.'[1]

Mark Coldridge, the liberal idealist, is closer to what she *had* been, shunning the messy human reality. We are able to see, too, in the larger cosmic context of the final book that the surrounded city has become a symbol of the Western world hemmed in by the 'underdeveloped' Third World, the hungry shadow that threatens its sun. Looking back from this to Martha's gradually maturing awareness of the shadow city in the earlier books, we become aware of how the 'other town', 'Kaffir-town' in *Martha Quest* in the Zambesian town that is a small version of Johannesburg, is evoked in terms of the shadow metaphor.

As in the short stories, Lessing portrays her Africans with

---

[1] *FGC*, pp. 161–2.

scrupulous restraint, from the outside. With every slight appearance their presence slowly forms. This begins to acquire density in *A Proper Marriage*, though there are strong intimations toward the end of *Martha Quest*, notably Shilling's degraded dance at the Sports Club, dancing like the ape many secretly think him, for the white man's diversion, and the casual knocking down of the black man by the wedding car. In the second book Martha, stranded in a stifling suburban marriage at the centre of a mock foursquare city, is often an eye we see through, a receiver of impressions. She discovers herself a prey to false idealization: 'romanticizing poverty' when confronted with a poor black woman, a reaction that is only a reflex of her own uncomfortable ease, flirting with the appeal of Solly Cohen's communal household in a house in the coloured area which the *coloureds* have named 'Utopia', but which like most utopias is exclusive, only Jews need apply. She is all reaction: running naked and pregnant through the rain, flinging herself high-mindedly into the squalid streets of the Coloured quarter, a willed commitment and a failure – 'she had not been issued, as she had vaguely expected, with a completely new set of emotions'.[1] Meanwhile, on the fringe of these nervous white disorders, the drenched African workman plods homeward (no romantic wallowing in the rain for him), 'a group of Africans' pass by with 'a soft and distant look' or one waits, neat and orderly, at the Maynards' well-regulated table.[2]

Commenting on the series after the publication of the third book, *A Ripple from the Storm*, Walter Allen detected a change of direction: 'Martha Quest seems no longer the channel through which the action flows. . . . What had begun as a full-length portrait of a young woman has become a study of a society in process of disintegration.'[3] This is true so far as it goes, but if we consider *A Ripple from the Storm* in its place within the series we see that it is designed to be a trough in the uneven process of Martha's development.

This, her most politically involved period, is that in which she runs the most danger of losing herself, of losing grip of that private 'conscience' that had held her steady in earlier years. A wishful romantic idealism now distorts, not only her emotions, but those of

[1] *PM*, p. 358.
[2] *PM*, pp. 152, 251, 328. (Martha's dance in the downpour is, as has been pointed out, 'Lawrentian' – but the ironic context the contrasting 'native' life provides is not.)
[3] *Tradition and Dream* (Penguin, London, 1965), p. 297.

the 'revolutionaries' – of many shades – to whom she becomes attached. Her utopian vision, now fed by the seductive simplicities of Communist ideology, blurs the evidence of her eyes and her emotions: '. . . the future they dreamed of seemed just around the corner; they could almost touch it. Each [Martha and Jasmine] saw an ideal town, clean, noble and beautiful, soaring up over the actual town they saw, which consisted in this area of sordid little shops and third-rate cafés. The ragged child was already a citizen of this ideal town, co-citizens with themselves . . .' – the child is 'a small, bare-footed black child, pot-bellied with malnutrition': *he* little realizes it, but *they* know he is 'saved'.[1] The time will come.

In this euphoric state Martha moves dream-like through the degraded life around her. She can explain away her neurotic landlady, Mrs. Carson, tormented by fears of black marauders, as 'the product of a certain kind of society, and the Mrs. Carsons would cease to exist when that society came to an end'; with sublime faith she buttresses such solutions with her dream of life 'over there . . . meaning in the Soviet Union – over there it's all finished, race prejudice and anti-Semitism'.[2] Secure in her faith that utopia has been realized somewhere on earth, she becomes a naïve player in the shadow drama of a deluded revolutionary group who take their blueprints for the ideal society from the dry 'objective analysis' of the doctrinaire Communist refugee Anton Hesse (who becomes Martha's second, also inadequate, husband).

Objective herself, without overplaying the advantages of hindsight – she refrains from the Conradian irony the situation invites[3] – Lessing lets these impotent revolutionaries work toward their inevitable dissolution. There is room for compassion when, for example, the pathetically earnest working-class airman Jimmy, after fearfully forcing his indulgent comrades to pass a resolution 'that all people are equal, and that everything is a question of education'[4], breaks out of camp to carry his need to the 'native' location and commune with his theoretical brothers and sisters, only to be rebuffed at every turn by their fear and hostility. They call him 'baas', 'comrade baas', but the deepest betrayal is that of the petted African Elias, who turns out to be an informer; the price:

[1] *RFS*, p. 34.
[2] *RFS*, p. 27.
[3] Cf. Conrad's *The Secret Agent* (1907) and his assertion that 'ironic treatment alone would enable me to say all I felt I would have to say in scorn as well as in pity' (Author's Note).
[4] *RFS*, p. 129.

ten shillings. The airmen are 'posted' for inciting Africans to revolt.

Brotherhood is sound rhetoric, but it should not interfere with actual life, as Martha realizes when she goes out to a building site to speak to some of her idealistic friends among the trade unionists and finds each with his 'attendant African' scrupulously upholding the distinction between white (skilled, the 'baas') and black (unskilled, 'native') labour. Only the Greek Athen, that rare, truly loving Communist, lives out his conviction to the full and returns to his country knowingly to die for it. Athen would love his fellow-men whatever political label he took; in the rest political absolutism either reflects personal weaknesses and inadequacies or severely erodes the private life. In any case, in such a society Communism could only be an anachronism.

Landlocked, the fourth book, makes clear the essential divergence of black and white interests. This divides 'the African group of the Social Democratic Party' at its heart: though the whites in this inter-racial group are marked out as 'kaffir-loving' extremists by their fellow trade unionists, they are forced to realize how little truly loved they are by all but a few of the unequal blacks. This is sharply illustrated by the bitter confrontation that follows one of the study group meetings at which the Africans are to receive their education in the struggles of the working-classes to establish unions in South Africa:

> 'I take it,' said Mrs. Van pleasantly, 'that some of you consider these talks not useful?'
>
> 'No.' And 'That is not true,' from voices on the veranda.
>
> Another voice from the veranda said loudly: 'People who call themselves our friends. But they can only talk of the white people.'
>
> 'Shame!' said Mr. Matushi firmly, to the veranda.
>
> Athen said: 'Comrades, when the guns of the capitalists point at strikers, it is the same whether the strikers have black skins or white skins.'
>
> For a moment, silence, then the voice said from the veranda: 'Oh, quite the same! And also when the white men earn many times as much money as the black men.' A loud laugh, in which a great many people joined. Then the sounds of feet departing across hardened dust.[1]

The political groupings Lessing portrays in *Landlocked* are not

[1] *L*, pp. 132–3.

identical with those in Southern Rhodesia in the 'forties, but they have some basic similarities. The Social Democratic Party of the novel corresponds most closely to the Southern Rhodesian Labour Party, but that party was never 'Official Opposition to the Government'.[1] However, it would be fair to describe it as the 'unofficial' Opposition since both the Government Party and the Opposition Party in Southern Rhodesia during the period, each of which went under several successive changes of name, had an essential common interest in preserving European ascendancy. This common interest is focused in the novel by the highly organized national strike (probably suggested by the first general strike in 1948). It is a tragi-comic affair, whose absurdity is pointed on the one hand by the scene in which Mrs. Huxtable reproaches her ungrateful cook for 'planning to cut our throats', on the other by that in which Mrs. Van, the good socialist, instructs her own servants in strike tactics – only to be told by *her* faithful cook: 'I go only because my madam tells me to go. I think this is a wicked, wicked thing, and I do not understand it. God will forgive me.'[2] He is obviously an old-fashioned brand of mission boy. 'The white workers, in their roles as whites, had been alarmed and indignant. In their roles as workers, they had been impressed, and had even wished their black colleagues good luck as they went off.'[3] Their role as whites, the political action of the book brings us to the point of realizing, would predominate in the future. In this the 'opposition' and the Government were at one and together felt that they represented 'civilization'. 'In the late 1940s', writes a student of the Rhodesian situation, 'the Labour Party quickly lost support, partly because of internal disputes but more because its *raison d'être* disappeared as, with increasingly high standards of living, the identity of interests between European capital and labour became stronger than their differences.'[4]

Reading the third book and the fourth, aptly entitled *Landlocked*, is an oppressive experience. There is humour and compassion, but the record of human weakness, vanity and distrust is for long stretches akin to the objective exposure of an acute documentary. Yet in *Landlocked* Martha grows into a new fullness. She emerges

[1] *L*, p. 125.
[2] *L*. pp. 249, 258–9.
[3] *L*, p. 251.
[4] James Barber, *Rhodesia: the Road to Rebellion* (London, O.U.P., 1967), p. 10. (This view is explicitly endorsed by Anna in the African section of *The Golden Notebook*.) See also Shamuyarira, op. cit., p. 106 ff.

from the bleak purism of her early utopian phase through the engagement of her emotions by testing experience, not mere 'talking' of this 'problem' or that.[1] Her father's protracted dying forces her into a nearer contact with common human suffering than ever before. Striving more compassionately now against her revulsion from her mother, she learns to understand Alfred and May Quest, not as admonitory footnotes to a Marxist 'analysis' of bourgeois decadence, but as 'victims', like herself children of violence.[2] In this period of her life, struggling once more in the quicksand of family while the Communist mirage evaporates, Martha at last finds consolation 'through the golden gates of sex'. Thomas Stern, the Polish Jew, the man 'who would unify her elements' and 'be like a roof, or like a fire burning in the centre of an empty space',[3] puts her questing mind – and his own – at peace for a while. But as their love turns from a resource into a refuge they drift apart. Thomas later becomes Martha's surrogate and comes to stand for her in a relationship reminiscent of that in *Heart of Darkness* between Conrad's Kurtz and Marlow. He elects for the absolute, a pure dedication to a remote tribe whose ancestral home is later (as we learn in *The Four-Gated City*) obliterated by the floodwaters of the great Kariba Dam, and dies the classic death of the overwrought African Dreamer, scribbling Kurtz-like in his diary, 'vermin, vermin, we are all vermin'[4] – the conclusion of the ruthlessly self-probing idealist? If so, it isn't one for which Martha is yet ready, but later, in London, she will have her Yahoo anti-vision. Not yet having travelled as far as Thomas, she remains, wiser but still seeking, to reflect with growing detachment upon 'this country, her life . . . empty spaces through which people blew like bits of paper',[5] the city desiccated, the 'collective' life dispersed. She has a vision of the veld town returning to the dust it barely impinges upon and strains to come to terms with the fact that 'During five years of [her] time, of days when, for the most part, she had been bored, waiting for life to start, forty-four million humans had died, had been murdered by their kind.'[6] She abandons Zambesia to its Sergeant Tressell, Thomas's old enemy, the ubiquitous fascist; Thomas had said: 'The little clerks in power are

---

[1] *L*, p. 170.
[2] *L*, p. 203.
[3] *L*, p. 37.
[4] *L*, p. 279: Cf Kurtz's marginal scribble, 'Exterminate the brutes!'
[5] *L*., p. 164.
[6] *L*, p. 198.

dangerous. That's the German contribution to human know-ledge.'[1] Good-humoured, careless, self-indulgent, if Sergeant Tressell destroyed anyone, it would certainly not be himself. He is the most potent white figure we are left with, lording it in the Settlers' Parkland Hotel, built out in the bush close to the site of 'the last fearful battles of the Mashona Rebellion. . . . All this earth had been piled with the corpses of black warriors and a few of the corpses had been white, with names that appeared in history books and on monuments.'[2] Perhaps future history will tragically reverse this, by Africans, bitterly remembered slaughter – though by then, Sergeant Tressell will probably have emigrated to South Africa. If so, he will certainly not have been dislodged by those young white idealists who, as Martha leaves Zambesia, are about to repeat her fruitless efforts – only with their eyes directed toward the latest delusory earthly utopia, Communist China.

None of the four African novels of the series gives any very concrete intimation of the strength African nationalists were to wield from the mid-'fifties on. Naturally, it was harder for such movements to develop in the settled colonies than in those of West Africa which were governed only by a thinly spread Colonial Service. Lessing's African politicians are fairly representative of the range: Mr. Matushi has felt the benefits of white civilization in the missionary field and genuinely respects the sincerity of the Marthas, the Johnny Lindsays and the Mrs. Vans, but more portentous is the shadowy figure of Mr. Zlentli who is engaged in clandestine activity in the North – a more fruitful ground for agitation being the mine-workers in that part of Zambesia which would correspond to Northern Rhodesia. Such Africans are not central to her series,[3] but the 'native' is an ever present unknowable factor on the margins of these lives that attempt to preserve a total white insulation, as labourer, servant, sycophant or uneasily courted 'brother'. Some readers may remark the absence from Lessing's spectrum of the Christian Church organizations. The leader of the banned Zimbabwe African National Union, the Reverend Ndabaningi Sithole, though no sparing critic of the hypocritical white 'civilizing mission', has nevertheless praised the Church for its positive encouragement of African nationalism,

[1]*L*, p. 149.
[2]*L*, p. 141. The last 'native' uprising against the British South Africa Company's government was ruthlessly suppressed in 1896: the settlers recall it as an heroic battle for survival.
[3]Cf. the role of Mathlong in the African parts of *The Golden Notebook*.

through its teaching and preaching the significance of the individual and of brotherly love and its role in spreading literacy.[1] A less positive judgment has been made by another African Christian (and member of ZANU); Nathan Shamuyarira sees the Church's role as sadly ironic: 'the Church's teachings of equal human dignity before God provoked African desires for self-determination', but far too few missionaries were prepared to make the political connection – '[the Church] cannot support a qualified franchise, and the Land Apportionment Act, and still pose the question, "Who is my neighbour?" '[2] However this may be, it is a fact that the more forceful and demanding nationalist movements did not develop till the 'fifties, a period not covered by Lessing's writing; a revitalized ANC led the way in 1957, but was banned in 1959. (There are now, unfortunately, two rival groups, ZAPU and ZANU, both also banned.) Most of Lessing's Africans, including the mission-trained, belong to the older, more subservient generation Shamuyarira describes.

It would be inappropriate here to discuss *The Four-Gated City*, a book as long as its four forerunners put together, in all its aspects. In it, not only Africa, but specific time and place become subservient to Martha's striving for a cosmic vision, a vision that will both include and transcend her (our) historical moment. From London, 'the hub of the Empire',[3] inhabiting a Heartbreak House of English 'bourgeois' liberalism as housekeeper, mentor, guardian and sometime lover of its head, the utopist writer Mark Coldridge, she enters into a new kingdom of real community, as 'the person who runs things, keeps things going, conducts a holding operation'.[4] As I have pointed out in commenting on Martha's chastening response to Mark's vision of the city (quoted on p. 73), she brings to England the tempered realism of her colonial education, the painful lessons of a parti-coloured world. One ideal after another has failed her: in the light of twentieth-century history she realizes that 'the people' are anything but 'a well of strength and integrity'.[5] This she can now see objectively as a sad delusion in her English Labour Party friend Phoebe, the believer in 'the collective'; straining to love an

---

[1] See N. Sithole, African Nationalism (O.U.P., Cape Town, 1959).
[2] Op. cit., pp. 142–3.
[3] *FGC*, p. 35.
[4] *FGC*, p. 391.
[5] *FGC*, p. 526.

amorphous human mass, Phoebe abuses (like a good Communist) the literature of 'just personal emotions'.[1] It is these untidy, wearing emotions Martha now elects to serve, as if she were doing penance. The woman-centring man has also proved insufficient – 'men have ceased to be explorations into unknown possibilities'.[2] Alone again, beyond romanticization, she nevertheless finds herself paradoxically a centre for others, though she feels 'of all the times in her life she had never been less Martha than now'.[3]

As Martha grows in awareness and a willingness to cope with things as they are, she comes to regard her past life as the fragile vessel of the faintest intimations of higher possibilities of evolution. Her African life boils down to this:

> Her childhood had gone, except for small bright isolated events. For instance, she had once sat under a tree and looked across the veld and imagined a city shining there in the scrub. An ideal city, full of fountains and flowers. Like Mark's city. Perhaps the same city: but both, after all, were imagined. What had that stretch of country looked like? She could not remember, the blue mountains on the horizon stood up high into a cool blue sky, and they were streaked with snow. What had the house been like? It had gone. A shabby old grass-thatched house on a hill: but she could not see it. And inside? All gone. Even her bedroom which had once been her place, her refuge, and where she had known every brushmark on the wall, and how the separate strands of grass had glistened when the lamps were brought in. And after that, she had been married. She had lived in different places with Douglas Knowell. She had had a large house. She had had a daughter. Caroline had been a pretty small girl. She was now, what? Twelve? But that wasn't possible. And that long period (or it seemed so at the time) when she had been such an active busy communist and then an active and busy social person – what was left of it all? Anton. She could not remember the rooms where she had lived with Anton. Thomas. She could not remember his voice, could not hear it. What came back from Thomas was – the strong smell of fresh wet greenery, growth, a sound of strong rain hitting dust, the sun on a drenched tree.[4]

[1] *FGC*, p. 105.
[2] *FGC*, p. 335.
[3] *FGC*, p. 428.
[4] *FGC*, p. 243.

The idea of the city remains, and the memory of Thomas Stern, but battered, post-war London is no such city – that finds only allegorical existence in Mark's *City in the Desert* – and Thomas is dead. For the visionary condemned to live in time, history is a chaos he must either ignore or, certain of defeat, set himself to master. Martha, ever the striving idealist, adheres wearily to the latter course: the Korean War, the Kenya Emergency, MacCarthyism, Hungary, the Suez Crisis, the Aldermaston Marches in favour of Nuclear Disarmament – a rare experience of the warm, communal dream answered – nothing is wanting to convey the pressure of the 'public' upon the 'private' life.

Nor is the African 'problem' quite shed: the brief appearances of the black guests from Kenya at Mark Coldridge's dinner table serve to point out that colour prejudice is no uniquely colonial problem but alive in Britain – nor will idealistic literature solve it – 'To study law was more useful than to study literature when one lacked freedom. . . .'[1] Though a certain poignant relief is given by the African episode between the ageing Mrs. Quest and the black boy Steven whom her son and daughter-in-law give her as a personal servant, an example of the purifying possibilities of 'the personal relation', Mrs. Quest's discovery that she can be held to possess, in the best sense of the phrase, 'a black heart',[2] cannot dispel her lifelong paranoia toward the 'native' at large. Mrs. Quest's last unhappy confrontation with her daughter completes a rounded portrayal of a loveless yet warm woman whose best qualities are undermined by an ingrown fearfulness and distrust which Martha has come to see are not exclusive to the settler mentality. During the Aldermaston March, she reflects upon how many there had known war, how many lived under its shadow, how few were not somehow conditioned by violence:

> There were very few people indeed, in, or near or associated with these columns of walking people whose lives did not have a great gulf in them into which all civilization had vanished, temporarily at least. There was probably no one here whose life had, or could, be remotely like that one once described by Thomas as 'being born under the elm tree, living, courting, marrying, dying, being buried under the elm tree.'
> These were people who had all been stripped.[3]

[1] *FGC*, pp. 407–8.
[2] *FGC*, p. 288.
[3] *FGC*, p. 457.

'Sad', 'sensible', the students among them discuss the revolution radioactivity is already working, what will emerge in their children through mutation – 'What kind of capacity of brain, heart, imagination would be welcomed and what feared?'[1]

Soon after this, Martha embarks upon her own last quest into the 'new territory' to which she has been directed, not by the politically active Mark, but by his wife – the abnormal, deranged, mad or – to use R. D. Laing's more objective term – the 'ontologically insecure' Lynda. Her new journey within is an exploration of the Dark Continent of the human mind, her new Africa. At its most extreme – her confrontation with the self-hater, the self of the *race* – she follows Thomas ten years after into a Swiftian anti-vision of 'sleepwalking' 'defectively evolved animals'.[2] In tracing this new path, Lessing develops a sustained and intense inward rendering of Martha's perceptions and painful progress toward self-integration and her discovery of extra-sensory powers. Lessing takes for one of her texts of Part IV Idries Shah's description of the Sufi belief in the 'conscious evolution' of organs capable of transcending time and space,[3] and recruits in support of Martha's own success in moving toward this, not only the comparable experiences of Lynda, but such evidence as Thomas Stern's record of the old man's foreseeing, in the tribe Thomas died among, the flooding of their valley 'ten years before the Kariba Dam was finished and the valley flooded'.[4] Her new dream of possibility is contained in this plea:

> The civilized human race knew that its primitive members (for instance, Bushmen) used all kinds of senses not used by itself, or not admitted: hunches, telepathy, 'visions', etc. It knew that past civilizations, some of them very highly developed, used these senses and capacities. It knew that members of its own kind claimed at certain times to experience these capacities. But it was apparently incapable of putting these facts together to suggest the possibility that they were calling people mad who merely possessed certain faculties in embryo.[5]

[1] *FGC*, p. 458.
[2] *FGC*, pp. 553–6.
[3] *FGC*, p. 492. (Sufism is an Islamic form of mystical monism which has acquired, like Zen Buddhism, a certain appeal in the West. It has been popularized by Idries Shah, but the most reliable introduction is probably A. J. Arberry's *Sufism*, 1950.)
[4] *FGC*, p. 566.
[5] *FGC*, p. 573.

There can be no glib response to this: hardly anything less than the reader's willing immersion in experience comparable to Martha's will qualify him to judge. In terms of the novel's overall scheme, the effect is to confirm the stress upon an unremitting, lifelong exploration and testing of the potentiality of the self. Themes made much of in discussions of Lessing, of political engagement, women's 'liberation', the sex relation, are incidental to this – incidental, too, to a sustained commitment to the deliverance of humanity from the bonds of time, custom, history. At the end of the last chapter of the novel proper, we see Martha and Mark utterly isolated at an 'Establishment' party with a rightist tinge; she asks herself the question to which the answer is now self-evident:

> Where? But *where*. How? Who? No, but *where*, where. . . . Then silence and the birth of a repetition. *Where*? Here. Here?
>
> Here, where else, you fool, you poor fool, where else has it been, ever . . . ?[1]

'Somewhere', with all its imperfections, has finally prevailed over nowhere. Martha finally accepts the life her nature and circumstances have created for her. But Lessing renews the vision and completes Martha's life-history in an apocalyptic 'Appendix' which becomes a dystopian prophecy. The 'Appendix' is made up of a series of documents dated between 1995 and 2000, mainly written by Mark, his son Francis and Martha herself, summarizing the events which led up to the catastrophe and what followed it. The prior events include the founding of the fragile utopias men have always retreated into as bolt-holes from corrupt society or Armageddon. In the more idealistic sphere there is Francis Coldridge's community farm – a utopia 'without religious political or theoretical basis'.[2] More widely, as the signs become ominous even to the masses, there is an exodus from Britain that strangely re-enacts the era of African settlement, to set up 'little Englands' in North and East Africa: 'There is, now England has gone', Francis writes from a Rehabilitation Camp near Nairobi, 'an archetype of England'.[3]

These signs merely threaten to repeat sterile history. The only

[1] *FGC*, p. 645.
[2] *FGC*, p. 652.
[3] *FGC*, p. 671.

saving vision appears to be Martha's. Stranded upon an island to the west of Ireland she discovers amongst the new children who have survived this ultimate violence some with an inborn capacity to 'see' and 'hear'. This is a capacity for both telepathy and precognition, developed paradoxically, she speculates, as a result of a sudden shock dose of radiation. These children are 'grown up . . . mentally and emotionally . . . they are beings who include that history [of this century] in themselves and who have transcended it'; 'people like you and me' – she writes to Francis – 'are a sort of experimental model and Nature has had enough of us.'[1] He will understand, for he has already written to his stepdaughter that such powers as Martha describes bring new strength to 'the individual human conscience', but it will not quickly gain ascendancy, as the Catastrophe issuing from a narrative of cumulative disintegration has shown, over 'the dark side of the human imagination'.[2]

After Martha's death in 1997 or 1998, one of these exceptional children, Joseph Batts, leaves the island and comes within Francis' orbit in Africa; he is to become a gardener there, and it was the gardeners, we recall, who were the 'guardians' of Mark and Martha's ideal city in the desert. Thomas Stern, to love whom was 'time moving in one's breath',[3] was also a gardener. Joseph and the few like him must remain *hidden* guardians, for he is classifiable by a still backward rational psychiatry as 'sub-normal', fit only to work on a vegetable farm. To square the ten-year-old Joseph in every respect with those inhabitants of Martha's first envisioned city he is the child of miscegenation, his father black, his mother white. It is a vision to move, to enlarge our sense of the human mind's scope for a liberty we scarcely dream of – but we are left with two opposed interpretations: the last sceptical words of Mark, the worn-out idealist who can only ask what point there has ever been, or the faith in the future of the race and the possibility that its most highly evolved members and envisioned 'people from the sun'[4] may yet build a new earth carried on after Martha by his son Francis.

In this closing 'Appendix' to the series Lessing has surely brought it to a conclusion whose nature could hardly have been anticipated when it was begun the best part of twenty years before the final book appeared. This is not surprising, but it exposes one of

---

[1] *FGC*, p. 703.
[2] *FGC*, p. 677.
[3] *FGC*, p. 67.
[4] *FGC*, p. 698.

the dangers of the series novel, that later parts may seem to have been forced into conformity with an imaginative pattern projected at the outset. The 'Appendix' has this effect, though not *The Four-Gated City* proper: this is partly due to a certain arbitrariness of detail – the neat dovetailing of Joseph Batts with Martha's original vision, the return to Africa for the finale – partly to the sudden contraction of the time span into so few pages and to the need to establish nevertheless a convincing resolution of the *leit motiv* of the ideal city and to keep open some promise for the vital action of the individual conscience even after the dissolution of all established forms of community. The enormity of the task of making these aims, achieved as they are with means that assault readers' entrenched scepticism, leaves the work finally straining against the limitations of words to convey incommunicable experience. Furthermore, the bulk of the narrative has carried an oppressive freight of despair with *what is*, reminiscent in its images of oppressive enclosure (the city, its houses and rooms) of the Kafkaesque fiction of alienation Lessing has spurned: this cannot readily be offset, for the reader who must live here and now, with a faith in higher evolution.[1] Lessing's intentions remain positive, but if fiction is above all a rendering of the life we have, *The Four-Gated City* portends that Lessing's fiction is in danger of being starved out by her philosophy. Nevertheless, this close to the series is itself an opening into the new country of 'inner space fiction' that Lessing was about to explore in later works whose shape would be, unlike *The Four-Gated City*, in no way bound to fall into pattern with her previous writings.

[1]For a persuasive negative viewpoint see Frederick R. Karl, 'Doris Lessing in the Sixties: The New Anatomy of Melancholy', *Contemporary Literature* XIII, 1, (Winter 1972) pp. 15–33; Karl does not, however, pay sufficient attention to the positive aspect.

7 African Notes: The Golden Notebook

More so than *The Four-Gated City*, *The Golden Notebook* is only partly relevant to the subject of this study. It is by now well known as one of *the* most influential books concerned with the white woman's burden. It is less widely appreciated that, unlike such plainly purposeful works as Simone de Beauvoir's *The Second Sex* or Betty Friedan's *The Feminine Mystique*, it was not planned as such. This is so despite Lessing's disclaimers in numerous interviews since it was published in 1962, in her explicit Preface to the Second Edition (1972) – where she demonstrates roundly that 'this novel was not a trumpet for Women's Liberation' – and the abundant variety of the work itself. Like *Children of Violence* it fell hostage to the spirit of the time and to the critics' penchant for imposing an autobiographical reading on Lessing's works, doubly so this time because her protagonist, Anna Wulf, was herself a writer. In her Preface to the Second Edition, Lessing felt bound to make explicit the theme, which she had by then explored more fully in *The Four-Gated City*:

> This theme of 'breakdown', that sometimes when people 'crack up' it is a way of self-healing, of the inner self's dismissing false dichotomies and divisions, . . . nobody so much as noticed this central theme, because the book was instantly belittled, by friendly reviewers as well as by hostile ones, as being about the sex war, or was claimed by women as a useful weapon in the sex war.[1]

However, it is probably closer to her purpose to call this 'theme of "breakdown"' her *inner* theme: the outer, involving the novel's structure and the nature of its protagonist reflects her concern with the dilemma of the contemporary writer, portraying a writer who is

---

[1]Preface to *The Golden Notebook*, 2nd Edition (London, 1972). See also 'Footnote to *The Golden Notebook*', cited below.

not Lessing (Lessing creates her) but who reflects Lessing's constant preoccupation with the relationship between the writer and society.

In an interview printed in 1962, she spoke of her interest in 'the theme of the artist's sensibility as a mirror for our time', mentioning as its major explorers Joyce, Proust, Lawrence and Mann – whom she distinguished as 'the greatest of these'. She paid tribute to Mann's inimitable success in conveying the message that 'art is rooted in corruption – in illness, above all'. How could she go beyond what Mann had done?

> I felt that after that you should have a writer who can't write – that's the logical next step. If you're going to have a conscience about it, if you want to be a good human being, a humanist, you should say to yourself that you're not going to write. . . . The writer would say, 'It's bad to spend my time writing books because I ought to be doing something about the state of the peasants in somewhere. It's immoral to write when people are suffering.' Such a person would say, 'I ought to be developing myself as a person and not in this egotistical preoccupation.'[1]

Notice the conditional form of this statement: as Mann employed an ironic manner to avoid dealing with the subject too subjectively, so Lessing is anxious to make it clear that the narrative *persona* she uses should not be identified with herself. As Martha was, though no ordinary woman, a means of conveying typical experiences in typical situations, so Anna is a character in whose experience is crystallized what is, or should be, the plight of the socially responsible writer in our time. To employ a mythical counterpart invoked by Mann and others among his German contemporaries, Narcissus, the writer is by nature arrogant, and self-regarding; yet he may – still being human – feel the contrary impulse to turn outward and serve his fellow-men. In him, too, 'the individual conscience', of exceptional subtlety and complexity, must come to terms with 'the collective'.

These remarks suggest a kinship between Martha and Anna Wulf. The parallels are numerous: both feel a strong social idealism and would build the New Jerusalem after the Soviet model, but the 'great dream' fails them, both strain their bodies and spirits to the

[1] Interview with Robert Rubens, 'Footnote to *The Golden Notebook*', *The Queen's*, 21 August 1962, p. 31.

utmost in the quest for a humanistic wholeness,[1] both seek a fuller sexual relation than women have known before but not as a sole end – and there are several biographical links (compare, for example, Anton Hesse with Anna's Max Wulf/Willi Rodde); but the one is a writer, in the depths self-centred, the other sacrifices herself, as Martha does in middle and later life, to the needs of others. The writer must preserve at least a residual narcissism, or she would cease to write.

The writer's self-regard implies a degree of control, an ability to master his subject-matter in and through his medium: to make his world. This implies the possession of a philosophy; again, Mann is invoked by Anna as the last true novelist in this respect. All that can be written now is the documentary novel – 'we read *to find out what is going on*'[2] – a fragmentary report upon a fragmented world the writer cannot hold in a single vision. One of Anna's larger, personal fragments is her African experience: greatly different from Martha's in that it is unrooted, no native part of her sensibility, and therefore not easily assimilable in her life or art. She is seventeen when she goes out to Central Africa in 1939, as a tobacco farmer's wife, and leaves six years later, at the end of the Second World War. Thus, her African experience is contemporaneous with Martha's in Books Three and Four of *Children of Violence*. This means that the parallel is very limited: Africa is an episode for Anna, of which she can only make sense in the full perspective of her life; it is not part of an organically evolving experience.

In structure *The Golden Notebook* is not entirely original, though it is one of the most ambitious examples of its kind in English literature. In its departure from the conventional chronology of the traditional realistic novel, it is part of a trend which has become pronounced in modern fiction (though ever since the early history of the novel, there have been experimenters with narrative, notably in Laurence Sterne's *Tristram Shandy*, 1760–7). Joseph Conrad's *Lord Jim* (1900) and *Nostromo* (1904) were amongst the most innovative early modern novels. Conrad's collaborator, Ford Madox Ford, in his *Joseph Conrad: a Personal Remembrance*, commented on their shared revolt against the straightforward, chronological novel:

---

[1] See *The Golden Notebook* (Ballantine Books, New York, 1968), pp. 53, 190, 360. (All references to this paperback edition.)
[2] *GN*, p. 60.

It became very evident to us that what was the matter with the novel, and the British novel in particular, was that it went straight forward, whereas in your gradual making acquaintanceship with your fellows you never do go straight forward ... [*he goes on, to write of a fully developed fictional character*] you could not begin at his beginning and work his life chronologically to the end. You must first get him in with a strong impression, and then work backwards and forwards over his past.[1]

Ford himself carried out this technique in *The Good Soldier* (1915), but that was a rare performance before the twenties, when departures from the straight chronology became a general trend. Notable examples may be found from that period on in the work of Joyce, Woolf, Huxley and Lowry, and the Americans, Fitzgerald, Faulkner and Dos Passos (to name only a few). Perhaps the most extreme example of the use of distorted chronology, B. S. Johnson's *The Unfortunates*, was recently published in England (1969): it is divided into twenty-seven sections, of which only the first and last are numbered, the remainder may be read in any order the reader chooses. Distorted chronologies make exceptional demands on the reader's capacity for discerning the inner, essential order beneath the seemingly random juxtapositions of character, viewpoint and situation.

The Golden Notebook takes its shape from Lessing's dual intention: placing a writer who is herself a novelist at the centre of the work, to bring out the vexed complexity of the relationship between the work and the life, and to express herself in a form 'imitative' of the chaotic contemporary world – while at the same time transcending and ordering that chaos. A similar pattern had been used by André Gide in *Les Faux-Monnayeurs* (*The Coiners*: 1926): the discontinuous narrative was intended to imitate the 'untidiness' of life, while a novelist was also included as a major character, writing his own novel entitled *The Coiners*, living and creatively 'using' his experience within Gide's novel. This novel was behind the structure of Aldous Huxley's *Point Counter Point* (1928), which also contains a writer working on a novel in many ways similar to the one in which he plays a part; Huxley's Philip Quarles also keeps self-searching notebooks, though these play by no means so expansive a part as in Lessing's novel. Huxley's *Eyeless*

[1] *Joseph Conrad* (1924), pp. 129–30.

in Gaza (1936) is more ambitious – and confusing – in its use of chronological shifts and the shuffling of juxtaposed periods of time and incident to bring out, not a 'story', but the more philosophical and psychological aspects of the novel.

Clearly, Lessing inherited the example of such departures from the conventional norm and, like those, her novel is *designedly* fragmentary and only apparently chaotic. Those few critics who have complained that *The Golden Notebook* is an untidy receptacle for its author's unused notes and jottings are at least missing the fact that its structure was far from revolutionary for a novel of the 'sixties. While the interweaving of the parts is carried out with great skill, the novel's more individual qualities derive from the cast of the author's mind and the intensity of her vision. Here, apropos is Lessing's defence of the shape of *The Story of an African Farm*:

> The true novel wrestles on the edge of understanding, laying about on all sides desperately, for every sort of experience, pressing into use every flash of intuition or correspondence, trying to fuse together the crudest of materials, and the humblest, which the higher arts can't include. But it is precisely here, where the writer fights with the raw, the intractable, that poetry is born.[1]

The novel within a novel in *The Golden Notebook*, 'Free Women', Lessing has described as 'a skeleton, or frame . . . which is a conventional short novel, about 60,000 words long, and which would stand by itself'.[2] It is presented in instalments interspersed with extracts from four notebooks to convey the distance and disparity between what is experienced and what is written about – 'the short formal novel and *all this*'.[3] Anna herself comes to realize why she uses four notebooks, not one:

> . . . a black notebook, which is to do with Anna Wulf the writer; a red notebook, concerned with politics; a yellow notebook, in which I make stories out of my experience; and a blue notebook which tries to be a diary.[4]

By means of the Notebooks Anna 'divided herself into four' to avoid facing up to a chaotic experience; in one, the Blue, she tries to be

---

[1] Introduction to *The Story of an African Farm* (New York, 1976), p. 3.
[2] Preface to 2nd Edition, op. cit.
[3] 'Footnote to *The Golden Notebook*', op. cit., p. 32.
[4] *GN*, p. 475.

honest with herself, and it is this especially which is in the end superseded by the Golden Notebook, 'all of myself in one book'.[1] If we were to read the Notebooks entire, then 'Free Women', one novel by Anna the unblocked writer, we should trace the process of positive *re*-creation of experience: amongst the material that is not 'used' is her personal African experience, though that had been strong in Anna's memory and the source of intense emotion.

However, it does make an integral contribution through interplay between notebooks and novel to the larger scheme of *The Golden Notebook*. We learn at the beginning of the first Black Notebook entry that Anna had used her African experience profitably, to launch herself as a writer with a novel set in wartime Rhodesia, *Frontiers of War*, about a pathetic love affair between an English R.A.F. officer and a black girl; it was a successful early treatment of the 'colour problem', but Anna, remembering the experience out of which it was born, knows it isn't true. Looking back, her critical self disclaims it as 'an immoral novel' because of its 'terrible lying nostalgia'.[2] Her block derives partly from her sense of self-betrayal, her possession of false credentials as an important African writer; to exorcise the demon, she retraces the original experiences in memories and dreams. These occupy almost the whole of the first Black Notebook entry (pp. 64–153); a second incident is recalled at length in the Black Notebook (pp. 412–33), and several scattered references and reflections, many of them to do with the shameful, irritating success of her African fiction – or rather of the bowdlerized versions of it preferred by caricatured television producers and literary agents.

The first long passage recalls the experiences that revolve around the Mashopi Hotel, to which Anna, Max Wulf, the German Marxist refugee whom she later marries, Maryrose and the three R.A.F. officers who together compose a 'leftist' group retreat for week-ends of 'pleasure' – actually of considerable emotional turmoil. This passage, juxtaposed with the plot summary of Anna's Rhodesian novel *Frontiers of War* (pp. 57–9), exposes Anna's romanticization of her material, simplifying it for the sake of a facile artistic effect. Paul Blackenhurst obviously modelled for the officer in love with the African girl: in fact, he is portrayed as possessing the fashionable homosexual leanings of young Oxford men of the 'thirties, whose diffidence toward women is overcome by Anna's

[1] *GN*, p. 607.
[2] *GN*, p. 63.

forthright lovemaking. In the novel, Anna had transferred to him for greater 'romantic' impact the involvement with the cook's wife at the hotel of George Hounslow, an old-fashioned socialist, prosaic supervisor of natives at work on the roads, a diffident man who believes himself ugly but is actually very attractive to women. It is one of those practical arrangements, as we have seen, that a white man could carry on without incurring his fellow-settlers' wrath providing it wasn't advertised:

> . . . George had his affairs. And he liked African women particularly. About five years before he was in Mashopi for the night and he had been very much taken with the wife of the Boothbys' cook. This woman had become his mistress. 'If you can use such a word,' said Willi, but George insisted, and without an consciousness of humour: 'Well why not? Surely if one doesn't like the colour bar, she's entitled to the proper word, as a measure of respect, so to speak.'[1]

Neither Paul, who specializes in sardonic parodies of settlers' attitudes, nor George is well suited to the reader's conventional expectations. George's agonized conscience over the fact that the half-caste children he has fathered will not have equal opportunity with those of his own marriage – 'it's the responsibility. It's the gap between what I believe and what I do' – expose *his* contradiction, between his socialism and his desire for women. This is hardly the stuff of sensational fiction, so Anna had transposed it into a confrontation between the heroic handsome alien and the Yahoo settlers. Among the latter would have been cast Mrs. Boothby, the hotelier's hard-pressed wife, butt of Paul's provocative indulgence of the cook:

> But looking back I see Mrs. Boothby as a lonely, pathetic figure. But I didn't think so then. I saw her as a stupid 'aborigine'. Oh, Lord, it's painful thinking of the people one has been cruel to.[2]

What is recalled, then, is a complex of entangled lives and emotions which Anna failed to render into art, not because her art should have been a more literal copy, but because her art was false to the depths of her experience – as, for example, the passage in which with great delicacy of feeling her lovemaking with Paul is

[1] *GN*, p. 127.
[2] *GN*, p. 142.

remembered and the aftermath, as they sit before the cave whose wall is covered with Bushmen paintings 'white oafs' have stoned for amusement.[1] Nevertheless, re-reading this first Mashopi Hotel memory some months later, Anna feels it still lacks 'objectivity' and that, though an utterly different story, it shares with *Frontiers of War* the weakness of 'nostalgia'.[2]

Both pieces are flawed by excessive subjectivity: *Frontiers* by sensation-seeking, the Notebook entry by too passionate an attachment to the emotional experience. In the first Yellow Notebook entry we follow an attempt by Anna to write another novel, *The Shadow of the Third*, that will reshape recent experience more objectively; she concludes:

> Literature is analysis after the event.
> The form of that other piece, about what happened in Mashopi, is nostalgia. There is no nostalgia in this piece, about Paul and Ella, but the form is a kind of pain.[3]

Either approach is costly to the person behind who creates. Capering always in the background are the spectres of world anarchy and violence, whose African contribution is Mau Mau and the Kenya Emergency. Her compensating dreams paint fantasies of wholeness, a richly diverse coloured world but one:

> Africa was black, but a deep, luminous, exciting black, like a night when the moon is just below the horizon and will soon rise.[4]

Such visions, she knows, are wishful projections into an unforeseeable future. Yet they are acts of faith which, morally responsible writer that she is, she wishes to make if she can do so sincerely. It is from this viewpoint that an African theme enters the novel, 'Free Women'. It does so in a shape that significantly differs from the subjective Mashopi experiences.

In 'Free Women: 3' Anna's friend Molly and her son Tommy, who had after reading Anna's depressing notebooks unsuccessfully attempted to commit suicide and blinded himself, form a close-knit triangular relationship of attraction and antagonism. After the suicide attempt, Tommy turns to his father's neglected second

[1] *GN*, pp. 148–50.
[2] *GN*, p. 153.
[3] *GN*, p. 228.
[4] *GN*, p. 298.

wife, Marion, and together they seek renewed purpose in dedication to the good of others. They light upon the fashionable cause of African freedom and ask Anna for the name of an imprisoned African nationalist leader she had known, to whom amongst others they intend to write encouraging letters of support.[1] Anna is sceptical about the practical value or sincerity of this scheme of Tommy's, but the leader in question, Tom Mathlong, is to reappear in 'Free Women' and assume central importance in the shaping of Anna's *credo* as a writer. However, before this happens, Anna's next Black Notebook memory of Mashopi is aptly juxtaposed.[2] Touched off by a man's absurd, accidental killing of a pigeon in Trafalgar Square (where they are held almost sacred), the pigeon-shooting episode near Mashopi Hotel is itself fraught with circumstantial ironies. Africa's indifferent, prodigal nature supplies them, for good measure in two utterly opposed symbolic forms: blindly mating myriad grasshoppers on the one hand, on the other 'a million white butterflies with greenish-white wings'. This festival of fertility, purposeful, blind, unceasing – and destructive – is an ironic setting for the group of people whose sexual sparring and innuendo and destructive tension seems little more than a subtle variant on an amoral natural law. Of course, the players in the episode are themselves sophisticated enough to see such ironic links, as when Paul praises 'this country' for educating him and the nicely brought up Jimmy 'into the realities of nature red in beak and claw', while his own careless dominance over the miserably worshipping Jimmy seems little more than an extreme refinement upon the relationship between the ant-eater and the ant. Human beings are also animals that think: while lacerated feelings burn hopelessly, Paul discourses with acute foresight on 'the reality of our time' that the future holds, when the veld will be covered with neither grasshoppers nor butterflies but 'semi-detached houses filled by well-clothed black workers', the mass society of an industrialized Africa, whether socialist or capitalist. He asks whether this will be preferable to 'the simple savagery of the Matabele and the Mashona' (they are sitting near some old barricades erected by the Mashona in the last tribal wars before the whites came). Clearly, this memory comes closer to Anna's perspective as a recorder of violent and meaningless human history:

[1] *GN*, p. 400.
[2] *GN*, pp. 412–33: The remaining quotations in this paragraph are taken from these pages.

an 'objective' effect emerges from an intense personal experience – but it only does so if seen in combination with the other fragments the notebooks supply. It, too, is left out of 'Free Women', but we know – because we have both – how it helped to form the continuation of the African theme in Anna's novel.

There, Paul's pessimistic vision of black Africa is implicitly tempered (at least) by the meaning of Mathlong. He reappears in 'Free Women: 4', though briefly and only in Anna's memories, as a firmly realized figure of realism and genuine purposefulness. Anna imagines him laughing indulgently at the sentimental concern of Tommy and Marion or the students who riot on behalf of him and his kind, 'out of a private need to challenge and to be punished by authority';[1] she remembers him on the Thames river boat feeling, as they passed Westminster, 'the weight of the British empire like a gravestone',[2] not because it had made him suffer but because of his sober sense of the seemingly infinite time it would take to build in Africa a unity and order comparable to Britain's. Her feeling for him betrays her into enthusing about him to Marion as 'a sort of saint',[3] but she hits a sharper note when she unsettles Marion by telling her that African politics can be likened to those of Elizabethan England: the sentimentalist cannot bear even such remote parallels with white civilization. This passage in 'Free Women' is juxtaposed against a further brief Mashopi entry when the Black Notebook is resumed: after a number of newspaper cuttings, every one of which 'referred to violence, death, rioting, hatred, in some part of Africa', a dream follows, inspired by the television producer's suggestion that Anna's novel *Frontiers of War* should be shot on location: the cameras are all trained on the white cast by black cameramen. The cameras are also machine guns: Anna thinks it a dream of 'total sterility'.[4]

The Notebook narrative now traces Anna's accelerating slide into disolution, every nerve rubbed raw by her new affair with the American Saul Green, the loved antagonist who is painfully forcing her to feel and suffer again. Seeking strength in remembering Africa (a retreat from the present) her mind supplies, not Mathlong, but Charlie Themba, 'mad and paranoic, the man hated by the white men and disowned by his comrades'[5] – a casualty of the

---

[1] *GN*, p. 512. (Today this phenomenon has earnt the label 'radical chic'.)
[2] *GN*, p. 515.
[3] *GN*, p. 515.
[4] *GN*, pp. 524–5.
[5] *GN*, p. 593.

'Elizabethan' politics. It is easier for her to 'become' Themba; Mathlong stands apart, resisting, an exacting symbol of that state Anna herself must achieve, if she is to be the interpreter, not merely the passive victim, of the terrible history we all carry within us:

> ... this figure, unlike all the others, had a quality of detachment. He was the man who performed actions, played roles, that he believed to be necessary for the good of others, even while he preserved an ironic doubt about the results of his actions. It seemed to me that this particular kind of detachment was something we needed very badly in this time, but that very few people had it, and it was certainly a long way from me.[1]

In *The Golden Notebook*, in rough dream and deliberate recollection – the 'naming' process – Anna revisits Mashopi and, under the guidance of the 'projectionist' whom she identifies with Saul and then her 'conscience', comes at last to see her life straight, without 'making up stories' about it.[2] She emerges from the 'craziness' and incoherence of this agonising revision of values, no longer 'sunk in subjectivity',[3] but armed with 'a terrible irony, a terrible shrug of the shoulders, and it's not a question of fighting it, or disowning it, or of right and wrong, but simply knowing it is there, always'.[4] The transvaluation Anna achieves compels her behind her own experience into a humbling recognition that, for all her idealism, she has been a naysayer:

> The group under the gum-trees, for instance, or Ella lying in the grass with Paul or Ella writing novels, or Ella wanting death in the aeroplane, or the pigeons falling to Paul's rifle – all these had gone, been absorbed, had given place to what was really important. So that I watched, for an immense time, noting every movement, how Mrs. Boothby stood in the kitchen of the hotel at Mashopi, her stout buttocks projecting like a shelf under the pressure of her corsets, patches of sweat dark under her armpits, her face flushed with distress, while she cut cold meat off various joints of animal and fowl, and listened to the young cruel voices and crueller laughter through a thin wall. Or I heard Willi's humming, just behind

[1] *GN*, p. 597.
[2] *GN*, p. 616.
[3] *GN*, p. 614.
[4] *GN*, p. 634.

my ear, the tuneless, desperately lonely humming; or watched him in slow motion, over and over again, so that I could never forget it, look long and hurt at me when I flirted with Paul.

> ... the reason why I have only given my attention to the heroic or the beautiful or the intelligent is because I won't accept that injustice and the cruelty, and so won't accept the small endurance that is bigger than anything.[1]

When we turn to the final instalment of 'Free Women', the novel for which Saul has given her the opening sentence, we find this 'illumination' reflected as Anna's theme: the Anna she propels into her novel accepts that her need is to commit herself to social and political action, knowing full well the limited success that comes from pushing boulders against the 'great black mountain ... of human stupidity'.[2] Not for her the top of the mountain where stand the great who have always known the essential truths: this motif, saved from the incomplete Yellow Notebook novel, *The Shadow of the Third*,[3] can now be transferred from the simpler Ella and integrated into Anna's cleansed outlook. Like Mathlong, Anna has attained to an ironic sense of limitation which is not stultifying; it leaves her free to act, to express her need to be outgoing, and remain free from self-deception.

The reader may question whether in the undoubtedly 'Elizabethan' history of African nationalism there can be found a parallel to Mathlong that will strengthen one's desire to see him as no merely ideal creation. Mathlong's history is a representative one: like him, many leading nationalists completed their education in England and came to respect the political and social achievements of a country from which, nevertheless, they wished to be free, a country which, paradoxically, helped to feed their political thought and yet imprisoned them for seeking freedom. These include Julius Nyerere, now President of Tanzania, the late Tom Mboya of Kenya, the late President Nkrumah of Ghana, and Kenneth Kaunda, now President of Zambia (formerly Northern Rhodesia). Perhaps it was Kaunda Lessing had in mind. In two *New Statesman* articles, the second of which was written as a report on 'Zambia's Joyful Week' after Lessing had attended the country's Inde-

[1] *GN*, pp. 634–6.
[2] *GN*, p. 627.
[3] *GN*, p. 210.

pendence celebrations in 1964, her admiration for Kenneth Kaunda is marked: '[his] personality shines over everything. Zambia is lucky in his qualities, which are rare in a politician'.[1] In the earlier article, written before Independence, she had deplored Kaunda's imprisonment for 'being in possession of seditious literature' and regretted the gulf between such 'intelligent, well-informed and liberal' blacks and timid white liberalism.[2] Certainly, not all such men were Mathlongs – and recent African history has proved her right to doubt whether many such men could survive the cut-throat politics of Independence. However ideal he may be, Mathlong has a real enough counterpart: at present, much of Africa is in the hands of a type Lessing hardly needed to name such as Mathlong's 'friend – he's bombastic and rabble-rousing and he drinks and whores around. He'll probably be the first Prime Minister – he has all the qualities – the common touch . . .'[3] Taking over where Lessing leaves off, several black African novelists have characterized this type with an inward understanding no white writer could achieve – Chinua Achebe's *A Man of the People* and *The Beautyful Ones Are Not Yet Born*, by Ayi Kwei Armah, are notable examples. Peter Abrahams' *A Wreath for Udomo* is a flawed attempt to treat the theme of corrupted idealism. Also noteworthy is the implicit tribute paid Lessing's novel by Ayi Kwei Armah in his own *Fragments* (1970). Armah's anti-hero, a young African intellectual and idealist, is bitterly disillusioned on returning to his country after studying abroad and the novel traces his breakdown and disintegration into madness. As with Anna, the question is posed whether it is he who sees all too clearly or 'normal' society that is insane; Baako's reading during his breakdown is *The Golden Notebook*.[4]

The African element of *The Golden Notebook* discussed in this chapter accounts in length for no more than one-sixth of the whole novel, but it is crucial to our understanding of the book's theme; an analysis of the part it plays enables us to perceive the careful ordering of a novel which, contrary to some critics' views, is anything but a chaotic treatment of a chaotic subject. It also deepens our understanding of the significance of her primarily

[1] *New Statesman*, 6 November 1964, p. 692.
[2] 'The Kariba Project', 9 June 1956, pp. 647–8. (Kaunda has many admirers: Colin M. Morris writes in his Introduction to *A Humanist in Africa*, a selection of letters written to him by Kaunda, 'It is possibly [his] greatest attribute that he has shown that goodness can be attractive'. (Longmans, London, 1966), p. 10.)
[3] *GN*, p. 516.
[4] Ayi Kwei Armah, *Fragments*, Heinemann AWS edition (1975), p. 128.

African subject-matter by placing it in the widening, cosmic perspective to which, as we have seen, Lessing devotes herself completely in *The Four-Gated City*.[1]

[1] Perhaps the fullness with which this is done in *The Golden Notebook* may partly explain the great diminution in African material in Book Five of *Children of Violence*, but this is only speculation.

8   Conclusion

Since *The Four-Gated City* was published in 1969 Lessing has no longer been identifiable as an African writer in the strict sense, that is, her subject-matter is no longer African and her themes have no specific relevance to Africa.[1] She has published three novels since then, each of which develops the pattern begun by *The Golden Notebook* in that it is set in London or employs London as a focus and point of departure; except for the dream material, the setting and characters are English or European; the themes, however, are part of her continuing concern with the cataclysmic future she believes inevitable[2] – yet against which she continues to push her 'boulder' of warning. *Briefing for a Descent into Hell* (1971) pursues the exploration of what I have called her Inner Africa, in a powerfully imagined study in which a Professor of Classics in a state of amnesia, almost discovers the nature of his buried self before he is drawn back by the assaults of aggressive psychiatric treatment into 'reality'. He adds yet another to those Lessing protagonists who are not large enough to cope with the fearful promise of self-transcendence.[3] In *Summer Before the Dark* (1973) the protagonist is a middle-class Englishwoman, a 'successful' wife and mother of 45, outwardly in command of herself, inwardly empty and unsatisfied. During her husband's long absence on business, she travels in Spain, has an unsatisfactory affair with a young American, returns jaded to London and retreats (like Martha and Anna before her) into a claustrophobic, self-probing isolation. This, though

---

[1] Apart from two African stories, which are not among her most remarkable, included in *The Story of a Non-Marrying Man & Other Stories* (1972): the title story and 'Spies I Have Known'.

[2] 'I think the "iron heel" is going to come down. I believe the future is going to be cataclysmic.' Interview at Stony Brook, N.Y., reported in *New American Review*, 8, January 1970, pp. 166–79 (after the publication of *The Four-Gated City*).

[3] I have reviewed this novel at length in *Encounter* (September 1971) and *The Journal of Commonwealth Literature* (June 1972).

necessary, is against her nature: she abandons self-concern in a compassionate awakening to the plight of the young and weak whom she finds herself lodging among, young without purpose or saving illusion – a further lapse from the at least *active* recognition of the young Aldermaston marchers in *The Four-Gated City*. From this novel, marred for one who has followed Lessing's work by a want of surprise, it seems a short step to Lessing's darkest projection into the cataclysmic future, *Memoirs of a Survivor* (1974). This novel, set in a broken London, in which order has finally given way to mass vandalism and mob-rule, fleshes out the nature of the disaster which was passed over rapidly in the 'Appendix' to *The Four-Gated City* for the sake of the prophetic aftermath. Readers of *Memoirs* who cannot pass through the door of extra-sensory experience that leads into Lessing's newly discovered other 'order of world altogether', will feel that the harsh future she convincingly imagines, far from being relieved, is rendered even more painful by the consciousness of so unattainable an alternative. These latest novels may not carry to all readers the conviction of a world view, unless one sees Lessing's doomed London as a symbol of the urbanized civilization that is disintegrating throughout the world. If she has African readers, it is hard to imagine that these visions set in the old world will distress them – but they may be mistaken. In any case, she has foreseen in the 'Appendix' to *The Four-Gated City* that with the final destruction of London (the old world?) Africa will be one of the two centres from which, for good or ill, life will continue; the other is China. . . . However, her belief in precognition and other forms of paranormal experience evident in all her books since *The Four-Gated City* is a turn of mind to which African rather than Western readers are likely to be receptive.

Western critics find a seeming irony in the latest developments of her work. I have earlier referred to her spurning in her 'manifesto', 'the Small Personal Voice', of the modern masters of despair, Beckett, Camus, Genet, and her counteracting allegiance to the great realists of the nineteenth century, Tolstoy, Balzac, Dostoievsky, Stendhal, and to Mann in our time, whom she praises for their 'humanity' and 'love of people'; they were writers capable of 'strengthening a vision of a good which may defeat the evil':

> In an age of committee art, public art, people may begin to feel again a need for the small personal voice; and this will feed confidence into writers and, with confidence because of the knowledge of being needed, the warmth and humanity

and love of people which is essential for a great age of literature.[1]

This was written over twenty years ago (1957); her African writing was in full spate, it contributed its force to many possibilities of imminent good – the freeing of Africa from empire, the exposure of racist attitudes while, at the same time, preserving an awareness of the common humanity of white and black. It was compassionate, constructive and timely work – but even then, as 'The Small Personal Voice' already acknowledged, it was overshadowed by 'the deep anxieties' and 'terrors' from which no part of the world was free, of nuclear destruction, mass poverty and hunger:

It is because it is so hard to think ourselves into the possibilities of the ancient dream of free man that the nightmare is so strong. Everyone in the world now, has moments when he throws down a newspaper, turns off the radio, shuts his ears to the man on the platform, and holds out his hand and looks at it, shaken with terror. The hand of a white man, held to the warmth of a northern indoor fire; the hand of a black man, held into the strong heat of the sun: we look at our working hands, brown and white, and then at the flat surface of a wall, the cold material of a city pavement, at breathing soil, trees, flowers, growing corn. We think: the tiny units of the matter of my hand, my flesh, are shared with walls, tables, pavements, trees, flowers, soil . . . and suddenly, and at any moment, a madman may throw a switch, and flesh and soil and leaves may begin to dance together in a flame of destruction. We are all of us made kin with each other and with everything in the world because of the kinship of possible destruction. And the history of the last fifty years does not help us to disbelieve in the possibility of a madman in a position of power. We are haunted by the image of an idiot hand, pressing down a great black lever; or a thumb pressing a button, as the dance of fiery death begins in one country and spreads over the earth; and above the hand the concentrated fanatic stare of a mad sick face.[2]

Some have accused Lessing of capitulating to this nightmare and adding her voice of despair to those others she had castigated in the

---

[1] *Declaration*, op. cit., p. 164.
[2] Ibid., p. 18.

'fifties. Yet her dark recent works are not, like Beckett's, shadow plays of vacancy. Whether or not one can take comfort from her vision of man evolving higher forms or developing paranormal powers (which seems to be the tendency of much dystopian writing) at the human level we know she has at least kept faith with the lesson Anna learnt, in 'the small endurance that is bigger than anything'.[1] Hers is still a 'personal voice' and while it remains so she will not lack listeners.

However her prophetic writing may be judged, and it is still evolving, we can assess her fifteen years' concentrated rendering and interpretation of her Africa (from *The Grass is Singing*, 1950, to *Landlocked*, 1965) as a complete body of work that will ensure her place as the most accomplished, versatile and illuminating white African writer in English we have seen, or are likely to see. Only the South African novelist Nadine Gordimer has produced work of comparable depth and, recently, of an intensity rivalling Lessing's; she has concentrated her artistic effects, eschewing the somewhat unequal breadth of Lessing's bildungsroman, *Children of Violence*. It has been said that all major literature is regional, so deeply rooted in intense 'local' experience that it reaches down in the course of nature to the universal. Lessing's strength largely stems from her being truly an African writer in this sense, a writer Africa made. Her passionate psychic and physical response to Africa contributed that romantic 'conscience' which blends, most unusually in a modern writer, with a more contemporary analytical social and psychological realism. It is a tragic literature because what is most loved must also be lost: 'All white-African literature', she has written, 'is the literature of exile: not from Europe, but from Africa'.[2] It is possible that everything she has written since she left Africa, not only her African writing, is the voice of such an exile. Yet the last word should be that her African writing is not limited by the word 'African': because she never yielded to the temptation to treat the 'colour problem' simplistically, but kept instead a clear, compassionate eye upon the humanity of all she portrayed, her work transcends the relatively brief episode of white settlement and places it in firm perspective as one of the seemingly tragic histories of universal distrust and hostility between races, creeds and classes. So long as the fragmented world evades cataclysm, her African witness will be an enduring resource for those who still hope to make it one.

[1]*GN*, p. 636.
[2]Book review, 'Desert Child', op. cit., p. 700.

Bibliography

(Place of publication London, unless stated otherwise.)

Doris Lessing

I Separate Works (in order of publication)
The Grass is Singing, Michael Joseph, 1950. Penguin Books (paperback), 1961. (Novel)
This Was the Old Chief's Country, Michael Joseph, 1951. (Short Stories)
Martha Quest, Michael Joseph, 1952. Panther Books (paperback), 1966. New York, Simon & Schuster, 1964. (Novel)
——'Children of Violence', Book 1.
Five, Michael Joseph, 1953. Penguin Books (paperback), 1960. (Five short novels: 'A Home for the Highland Cattle', 'The Other Woman', 'Eldorado', 'The Antheap', 'Hunger'.)
A Proper Marriage, Michael Joseph, 1954. Panther Books (paperback), 1966. New York, Simon & Schuster, 1964. (Novel)
——'Children of Violence', Book 2.
Retreat to Innocence, Michael Joseph, 1956. Sphere (paperback), 1967. (Novel)
The Habit of Loving, MacGibbon & Kee, 1957. New York, T. Y. Crowell Co., 1957. (Short Stories)
Going Home, Michael Joseph, 1957. Drawings by Paul Hogarth. Revised edition, Panther Books (paperback), 1968. (Personal narrative)
A Ripple from the Storm, Michael Joseph, 1958. New York, Simon & Schuster, 1966. (Novel)
——'Children of Violence', Book 3.
Each His Own Wilderness, in *New English Dramatists*, *Three Plays*, introduced and edited by E. Martin Browne, Penguin Books (paperback), 1959.
Fourteen Poems, Scorpion Press, 1959.
In Pursuit of the English: A Documentary, MacGibbon & Kee, 1960. New York, Simon & Schuster, 1961. Sphere (paperback), 1968. (Personal narrative)

The Golden Notebook, Michael Joseph, 1962; New edition, with Author's Preface, 1972. New York, Simon & Schuster, 1962. Penguin Books (paperback), 1964. (Novel)

Play With a Tiger: A Play in Three Acts, Michael Joseph, 1962.

A Man and Two Women, MacGibbon & Kee, 1963. New York, Simon & Schuster, 1963. Panther Books (paperback), 1965. (Short Stories)

Landlocked, MacGibbon & Kee, 1965. New York, Simon & Schuster, 1966. Panther Books (paperback), 1967. (Novel)
——'Children of Violence', Book 4.

Particularly Cats, Michael Joseph, 1967. New York, Simon & Schuster, 1967. (Personal narrative)

The Four-Gated City, MacGibbon & Kee, 1969. New York, Knopf, 1969. (Novel)
——'Children of Violence', Book 5.

Briefing for a Descent into Hell, Jonathan Cape, 1971. New York, Knopf, 1971. (Novel)

The Story of a Non-Marrying Man & Other Stories, Cape, 1972. Published New York, Knopf, as *The Temptation of Jack Orkney & Other Stories*, 1972. (Short Stories)

The Summer Before the Dark, Cape, 1973. New York, Knopf, 1973. (Novel)

Memoirs of a Survivor, Octagon Press, 1974. New York, Knopf, 1975. (Novel)

II Collected and Selected Works

African Stories, with Author's Preface, Michael Joseph, 1964. New York, Simon & Schuster, 1965.

Nine African Stories, selected from *African Stories* by M. Marland, with illustrations, Longmans, 1968.

This Was the Old Chief's Country, Volume One of Doris Lessing's Collected African Stories, with a new Author's Preface, Michael Joseph, 1973.

The Sun Between Their Feet, Volume Two of Doris Lessing's Collected African Stories, with Author's Preface, Michael Joseph, 1973.

III Occasional Publications (* signifies items of African interest)
(a) *Articles; Parts of Books:*

*'Myself as Sportsman', *New Yorker*, XXXI, 21 January 1956, pp 78–82.

*'Being Prohibited', *New Statesman*, 21 April 1956, pp. 410–12.

*'Kariba Project', *New Statesman*, 9 June 1956, pp. 647–8.

'The Small Personal Voice', in *Declaration*, ed. T. Maschler, MacGibbon & Kee, 1957. (Gives her 'position' as writer.)

'London Diary', *New Statesman*, 22 March 1958, pp. 326–7, 367–8.

*'Crisis in Central Africa, The Fruits of Humbug', *Twentieth Century*, 165, April 1959, pp. 368–76.

'Ordinary People', *New Statesman*, 25 June 1960, p. 932.

'Smart Set Socialists', *New Statesman*, 1 December 1961, pp. 822–4.

'What Really Matters', *Twentieth Century*, 172, Autumn 1963, pp. 96–8.

*'All Seething Underneath', *Vogue*, 15 February 1964, pp. 80–1.

*'Zambia's Joyful Week', *New Statesman*, 6 November 1964, pp. 692, 694.

*Afterword in *The Story of an African Farm*, by Olive Schreiner, Fawcett Publications (Connecticut), 1968, pp. 273–90.

Reprinted in a new edition of *The Story*, Schocken Books (New York), 1976, pp. 1–18.

'A Few Doors Down', *New Statesman*, 26 December 1968, pp. 918–19. (On colour prejudice in London.)

'An Ancient Way to New Freedom', *Vogue*, 158, July 1971, pp. 98, 125, 130–1.

Foreword to *An Ill-Fated People, Zimbabwe Before and After Rhodes*, by Lawrence Vambe, Heinemann, 1972. pp. xiii–xxi; also published by University of Pittsburgh Press, 1973.

'In the World, Not of it', *Encounter*, Vol. XXXIX, ii, August 1972. (An article on Sufism.)

'The Ones Who Know', *The Times Literary Supplement*, 30 April 1976, pp. 514–15: a review of several books on Sufism.

(b) *Interviews*

'Footnote to *The Golden Notebook*', interview by R. Rubens, *The Queen*, 21 August 1962.

Interview by R. Newquist, *Counterpoint*, New York 1964.

'Talk with Doris Lessing', excerpts from interview by Florence Howe, *The Nation*, 204, 6 March 1967, pp. 311–13; printed in full as 'A Conversation with Doris Lessing (1966)' in *Doris Lessing: Critical Stories* (ed. Pratt and Dembo), University of Wisconsin Press, 1974, pp. 1–19.

'Doris Lessing: Cassandra for a Century of Catastrophes', interview by Joseph Haas, *Chicago Daily News*: Panorama, 14 June 1969.

'Scenarios of Hell', interview by L. Langley, *Guardian Weekly*, 24 April 1971.

C. J. Driver, 'Profile 8: Doris Lessing', *The New Review*, Vol. 1, No. 8 (November 1974), pp. 17–23: though by a South African novelist in exile who 'knew various members of her [Lessing's] family (daughter, brother, sister-in-law) and had lived for a while in Rhodesia', it is – by the subject's request – not a 'personal' article. Nevertheless, it undercuts several loose assumptions about autobiographical aspects of her fiction.

(c) *Reviews:*

*'Desert Child', *New Statesman*, 56, 15 November 1958, p. 700. [Rev. *The Lost World of the Kalahari*, by Laurens Van Der Post.]
*'African Interiors', *New Statesman*, 62, 27 October 1961, pp. 613–14. [Rev. *The Heart of the Hunter*, by Laurens Van der Post.]
'An Elephant in the Dark', *Spectator*, 213, 18 September 1964, p. 373. [Rev. *The Sufis*, by Idries Shah, Introd. Robert Graves.]
'Allah Be Praised', *New Statesman*, 71, 27 May 1966, pp. 776, 778. [Rev. *The Autobiography of Malcolm X*, with Alex Haley.]
'What Looks Like an Egg', *New York Times Book Review*, 7 May, 1972, p. 6.

(d) *Poems:*

'Here', *New Statesman*, 71, 17 June 1966, p. 900.
'A Visit', *New Statesman*, 72, 4 November 1966, p. 666.
'Hunger the King' and 'A Small Girl Throws Stones at a Swan in Regent's Park', *New Statesman*, 74, 24 November 1967, p. 731.
A note on editions cited in the text: I have, where possible, cited the most accessible paper back editions throughout (e.g., Penguin and Panther books).

Some Books of Related Interest

James Barber, *Rhodesia: The Road to Rebellion*, London: O.U.P., 1967.
A scholarly study of the origin and course of the events leading up to the Rhodesian Front Government's Unilateral Declaration of Independence (U.D.I.) in 1965.

Karen Blixen (Isak Dinesen), *Out of Africa*, London: Putnam, 1937; Cape paperback 1964.
African memoirs of the Danish novelist who managed a coffee plantation in Kenya from 1913 to 1931: of an earlier generation,

Blixen shows no comparable political awareness, but her sensitivity to the African landscape is strongly akin to Lessing's; in her Introduction to an edition of *The Story of an African Farm* she links this suggestively with the feminine sensibility.

Larry W. Bowman, *Politics in Rhodesia*: White Power in an African State, Cambridge, Mass.: Harvard U.P., 1973. Analyses evolution of white supremacist regime as the product, not of the crisis of the 1960s, but of a consistent pattern beginning with the early European settlement of the 1890s.

The Story of Kingsley Fairbridge, by himself, London: O.U.P., 1927.
Fairbridge was responsible for bringing numerous orphans out from England to a new life in Rhodesia; his vision is a curious example of a white humanitarian's one-eyed philanthropy: 'I saw waste turned to providence, the waste of unneeded humanity converted to the husbandry of *unpeopled* [my italics] acres'.

Lewis H. Gann, *Central Africa: the Former British States*, Englewood Cliffs, N.J., Prentice-Hall, 1971.

Kenneth Kaunda, *A Humanist in Africa*, London: Longmans, 1966.

Philip Mason, *The Birth of a Dilemma: the Conquest and Settlement of Rhodesia*, London: O.U.P., 1958.

Ezekiel Mphaphlele, *The African Image*, London: Faber & Faber, 1962; 2nd Edition (revised), 1974.
A wide-ranging socio-literary study of African 'personality', nationalism, black-white relationships, by a black South African now living in exile in the United States.

Gertrude Millin, *Rhodes*, London: Chatto & Windus, 1933.
——, *The South Africans*, London: Constable, 1926; 2nd Edition, 1934.

E. D. Morel, *The Black Man's Burden: the White Man in Africa from the Fifteenth Century to World War I*, 1920; reprinted, London and New York, by Monthly Review Press, 1969.
A pioneering exposure of 'the atrocious wrongs which the white people have inflicted upon the black'.

Charles L. Mungoshi, *Waiting for the Rain*, Heinemann, AWS, 1975: a sensitive and revealing novel of Shona village life in

Rhodesia, including the themes of social change and of division between the conservative old and the young who move out into unrooted urban life and life abroad.

T. O. Ranger, *The African Voice in Southern Rhodesia 1898–1930*, London: Heinemann, 1970.

Ronald Robinson and John Gallagher, with Alice Denny, *Africa and the Victorians: The Official Mind of Imperialism*, London: Macmillan, 1961.

Stanlake Samkange, *The Mourned One*, Heinemann, AWS, 1975: a novel of social protest, set in 1935, centring upon the judicial murder of an African convicted of a white woman's rape; this is fiction, but revealing and sometimes vivid in its depiction of a society which has changed little since 1935.

Olive Schreiner, *The Story of an African Farm*, 1883 (Penguin Books 1971).
——, *Trooper Peter Halket of Mashonaland*, London: T. F. Unwin, 1897.
A hastily conceived novel written to denounce Rhodes's Chartered Company's slaughter of the Mashonas in 1896: more a visionary act of moral denunciation than a work of fiction.
——, *Olive Schreiner: a Selection*, edited by Uys Krige, Cape Town and London: O.U.P., 1968.

Nathan M. Shamuyarira, *Crisis in Rhodesia*, London: Deutsch, 1965.
An attempt 'to describe the rise and growth of the African nationalist movement [in Southern Rhodesia] between the years 1955–64' by the former editor of *The African Daily News* (Salisbury), 1956–63.

Ndabaningi Sithole, *African Nationalism*, Cape Town and London: O.U.P., 1959.
By the leader of the Zimbabwe African National Union, one of the two (banned) Nationalist parties in Southern Rhodesia; he was jailed or 'under restriction' from 1965 to 1977, when he was invited to negotiate with the Smith regime.

Robert Blake, *A History of Rhodesia*, London, Eyre Methuen, 1977.

Lawrence Vambe, *An Ill-Fated People, Zimbabwe Before and After Rhodes*, Heinemann, 1972.

110

'A personal point of view of the Rhodesian situation' by the great-grandson of Mashonganyika, the Paramount Chief of the Mashona tribe who was executed after the Mashona uprising in 1896. Drawing upon tribal lore and verbal tradition, Vambe aims to correct the distortions of European historians who have characterized his people as 'primitive' and 'cowardly', a myth perpetrated since Rhodes' time to justify the view that 'the Shona people throughout Zimbabwe were hapless victims of Ndebele (Matabele) savagery, from which they were gratefully delivered by white men'. In her Foreword, Lessing welcomes Vambe's exposure of the whites' self-serving myths – upon which she herself had been reared. If not wholly convincing in its sometimes ideal view of his own people, Vambe's history gives overall a far more plausible version of Mashona reaction to the coming of 'the Pioneers'.

Index

9